OVERCOMING TOXIC RELATIONSHIPS

NAVIGATE THROUGH YOUR RECOVERY
WITH CONFIDENCE, PREVENT FUTURE
EMOTIONAL HARM, BUILD HEALTHIER
INTERPERSONAL CONNECTIONS, AND
LEARN TO BREATHE AGAIN

L C. QUINN

PREFACE

Hi there, and welcome to my book. I'm excited to share this journey with you. Let me give you a bit of background about myself and why I felt compelled to write this book.

I completed my bachelor's degree in criminal justice with a minor in psychology at the University of Saint Martin's in Washington State in 2013. My curiosity about how our minds work has always driven me. During my undergrad years, we participated in "ride-alongs" with police officers, where we were exposed to domestic violence cases and the toxic traits of others. At the time, it was "just" an experience, but as I progressed in my career, I realized that toxicity was a much bigger issue than I initially thought. After graduation, I joined the workforce and could better recognize the toxicity in relationships, not only in my own experiences but was continuously a lending ear to many of my friends.

My growing interest in the human mind led me to pursue a master's degree in *human relations* from the University of Oklahoma in 2018. While most of my studies focused on human relations in the workforce, it soon became apparent that understanding these dynamics also opened the door to examining how people deal with toxicity in all types of relationships. This book explains why acknowledging toxic traits in others is so important for your overall well-being. It is aimed at helping people recognize and overcome toxicity in various types of relationships. I hope this book gives you the insight and tools to navigate these difficult situations.

As I strive to reach more readers, I am deeply grateful for your time and consideration. I kindly request you to share your thoughts and experiences by leaving a review for my book. Your feedback is not just important; it is invaluable to me. Whether you found the book helpful, inspiring, or thought-provoking, your unique perspective matters. Thank you for your support and for being an integral part of this journey towards understanding and overcoming toxicity in relationships.

L. C. Quinn

CONTENTS

CHAPTER ONE

INTRODUCTION

I n the midst of a chaotic storm, it's hard to see beyond the swirling clouds and relentless downpours. Yet, when the skies finally clear, there's a moment of breathtaking clarity. It's in that stillness where you find your strength. No matter how broken or trapped you've felt, it's the glimmer of hope that pulls you through. That hope for a brighter, healthier future is what keeps you moving forward. Reflecting on your journey, you'll see that this hope guided you, even in the darkest times. If you're holding this book, chances are you're tired of being caught in the relentless cycle of toxic relationships, and you're ready to reclaim your life and your happiness.

What inspired me to write *Overcoming Toxic Relationships?* I wanted to make a meaningful impact and assure anyone navigating through difficult times that they are not alone. Through empathy, self-awareness, and personal experience, this book explores the complexity and emotional baggage that comes with toxic relationships. I wanted to provide a resource that can be relatable through practical, insightful advice and hope for anyone seeking to break free from toxicity.

As you dive into this book, I want you to harness its power

and use it as a step to heal from toxic relationships. Hopefully, this book guides you in learning how to improve your current relationships or build healthier ones. It's about unearthing, reacquainting with yourself, and enabling boundaries. As you flip the page, you will learn to identify the toxic patterns that have weighed you down. You will learn to recognize damaged relationships with family, coworkers, romantic partners, and friends. We will also laugh as we say goodbye to the negative self.

This book is for anyone who has felt stuck in a toxic relationship and is ready to break free. It will help you make sense of the madness, learn about the toxicity that has taken a toll on your life, and pave a way towards healing and loving connections. Through personal experiences and the latest research, you can use this book to grow emotionally and and break free from toxic relationships.

CHAPTER 1

THE ANATOMY OF TOXICITY: UNDERSTANDING ITS CORE

T oxic connections are a stark reminder of how deeply our emotional well-being can be affected by those around us. Maybe you've heard the saying, "Tell me who you hang out with, and I will tell you who you are." This phrase can be very relatable when deciding who we allow to enter our bubble. Relationships, whether with friends, family, or colleagues, are integral to our lives, yet toxic experiences can leave us feeling shattered and unsure of ourselves. Understanding these dynamics is crucial, as healthy relationships are essential for happiness and fulfillment. Have you ever noticed a shift in your personality when you are around negative people and vice versa when you are around people who act more fulfilled? As we go through this book, keep that in mind. Reflecting on our connections and striving to build healthier bonds with others is essential.

Defining Toxicity

The essence of toxicity can be defined through diverse manifestations of the toxic levels in relationships. Toxicity could be a spectrum of behaviors, actions, and thought patterns created to compromise another person's ability to live a fulfilling life. Thus, toxicity directly opposes mutual respect and understanding, which normal relationships rely on. It appears better suited to view toxicity as a parasite, which is often in need of lowering another person's self-worth. The core of toxicity is visible when a person is left incapable of seeing their value.

The Nature of Toxicity: Types of Toxic Relationships

Most often, the core characteristics of toxic relationships are manipulation, a striking lack of empathy, and a compulsive need to control. The lack of empathy is the essential quality of any human being, allowing people to understand each other, connect, and work together. In toxic relationships, a deep, yawning chasm of empathy separates partners from one another. People in toxic relationships often feel lonely despite living in the same house, becoming convinced they will always be misunderstood. The need for toxic individuals to control and possess is debilitating, causes insecurity, and pushes toxic people to dictate their partner's actions and limit their thinking.

Recognition Is Crucial

The effect of toxicity in relationships is disastrous. Relationships can be meaningless without empathy. Trust is at the center of all healthy and strong relationships, and its lack is the center of toxic ones. The manipulated person doesn't trust the manipulator but stays with them because of emotional attachment. The initial point for understanding something is wrong with someone close is learning to identify toxic patterns. Specifically, it is not about identifying abuses, which is often easy and direct, but rather understanding who is trying to control you, who is manipulating you, and who is not showing any empathy towards you. It would help if you learned to recognize these patterns so that, once identified, they allow you to consider working with that individual if they genuinely want to change or leave the toxic relationship and develop healthier connections.

You might not realize that you may be dealing with toxicity daily. Let's think of the following example: The supervisor at your office continuously undermines any input from your side, dismisses your issues without consideration, and takes control of your everyday work activities to the extent of denying your participation. All these aspects can be regarded as signs of toxic behavior, which some people can avoid or fail to notice. Still, it is crucial to understand that such behavior is not about your work or merits but of toxic nature.

Such a scenario may be familiar to many, but it's important to remember that it's not about the employees' competence. It's about the need for change. Creating a work environment where respect, freedom, and independence thrive can be a challenge. However, it's crucial to recognize and accept that such toxic environments in the workplace are characterized by specific attributes or signs that should be identified. Once these signs are learned, it's up to us to take the initiative and develop alternatives that foster positive changes. This understanding can inspire hope and motivate us to strive for healthier, more fulfilling workplace relationships.

Signs You're in a Toxic Relationship: Beyond the Obvious

When I think about a toxic relationship, I don't focus on the obvious signs of abuse because they're pretty standard. Instead, I think about the subtle things many don't immediately notice. It's not about what's said but what's left unsaid. It's about promises that are always put off or feelings that are ignored. Neglect and indifference are like quiet warnings of toxicity—they might seem insignificant at first glance, but they're often the first signs of trouble.

Toxic behavior, subtly intertwined with our daily interactions, often goes unnoticed because of its understated nature, slipping by without our awareness. An example is when someone hides their critiques on advice by undermining the decision-making of others. Another example can be seen in the deliberate disrespect of personal boundaries, which perpetrators justify by a close relationship of kinship or love. Both examples are distinguished by their lowness of destructiveness that is not immediately evident in the relationship.

When the perpetrator invades the essence of personal space, it's like they're poisoning the air around them. The tension hangs in the air, making it extremely obvious, making every interaction feel like you're walking on eggshells. In toxic relationships, it's easy to feel like you are always bracing yourself for disappointment or being overlooked. Unsurprisingly, it can lead to feeling down and worthless, like nothing you do matters. Being trapped in such relationships can really mess with your emotions, leaving a sense of doubt in yourself.

The influence of toxic relationships is also a concern on the impact it has on self-image. Generally, toxic relationships imply a constant interplay between control, criticism, neglect, and periods of false affection and reliance on the other person, making it impossible to define themselves as a person with value and self-worth. The implanted self-doubt is, in a way, treacherous; it is equally pervasive, affecting the relationship in which it began and, as a consequence, one's professional and personal relationships. Blame and criticism leave you hesitant to express and defend your opinions or second-guess your decisions at any juncture. People may generally fear accepting and adapting to new opportunities, experiences, relationships, or engagements, waiting for them to fail once again.

When someone is stuck in a toxic relationship, they might hold onto tiny moments of kindness or hope that the other person will change. But those moments are like fleeting glimpses of light in a dark tunnel. It's like a mind game where there is hope for something better, but deep down, they know they're unhappy. It takes real courage to face a situation as such. Sometimes, it's necessary to look in the mirror and ask: Is this where I want to be? Is this what I deserve? It's tough because it means confronting the truth. But admitting that the situation is toxic doesn't always mean you've failed. It means you're ready to reclaim your dignity and move forward again.

The journey ahead is challenging, no doubt about it. But realizing that your options are limited can be a turning point. A moment of empowerment is when you start reaching out for help, setting boundaries, and making choices that pave the way for healing and growth. It's about embracing the lessons learned from dealing with a toxic relationship and becoming even more resilient.

Our brains are amazing, and the more we engage in specific scenarios, the more we can easily spot and view things a certain way. Most people learn to spot toxic traits without realizing it. Many believe it or not, have become increasingly proficient in distinguishing between healthy and unhealthy. They learn to stand their ground, hoping and expecting that the partner acknowledges the type of relationship they deserve. Their story is similar to the story of others, and the end is not just about surviving; it's about the discovery and constant internalization of a truth that taints their understanding of what it means to have a natural interaction with other humans.

Love, respect, and trust in relationships are the fundamental desires that drive us. They are not just something we would like to have but essential to our being. As humans, we often live and look for them in our lives. Toxic relationships teach us valuable lessons based on our ultimate fulfillment in relationships and what we shouldn't tolerate. Such can be conflicting and true when letting go can be one of the most challenging things we must do. What needs to be understood is that all relationships are a process of learning and growing. They can eventually teach us how to build healthier connections. As we deal with various manipulation techniques, the desires that drive us as humans must be at the forefront of our lives.

Gaslighting: The Invisible Manipulator

As far as gaslighting tactics, there are many, yet they all have one thing in common: their clear intent to blur and destabilize. Words such as "You are too sensitive" and "You are imagining things" are not attempts at verbal communication but jabs. These seemingly harmless statements, unnoticed by an outsider, actually undermine emotional or sensory reactions. They are meant to shift the balance of power in favor of the manipulator. The gaslighter doesn't just say things; they often act in contradiction, making their words seem like errors and further distorting the victim's perception of reality.

The long-term results of gaslighting are not less destructive than its ultimate instrumental purpose. People being manipulated fall into the trap of their doubts, stop believing in themselves, their memory, and their perception, and eventually lose a part of themselves. Such distrust, as subjective as it is, inevitably takes on an automatic character, which makes it difficult to leave. In most cases, the manipulator often goes out of their way to win any outside relationships the victim may have. The victim is usually deprived of the ability to make decisions on their own, to the point where they even wonder if they are going crazy. The world at this point is no longer the same. Where it used to be nice and sunny, it's now gloomy and has no way out. Reality is mixed in a dream, where understanding the truth is impossible. That's why the only way to solve this situation should be through the presence of a support system. This system should be based on the relationships of the affected person with friends, relatives, and acquaintances located beyond the gaslighter's circle of influence.

Therapy is undoubtedly the central part of the healing process from gaslighting. Having a professional to help you "fact-check" your reality and rebuild the lost trust in your perception enables you to develop different mechanisms and tools to fight the gaslighting. The dynamics of psychological and emotional manipulation help you begin the healing process safely and efficiently. It makes a whole difference when you find a therapist who understands gaslighting, as they help you get out of your comfort zone and open up every layer of your deception. Therapists provide a safe place for you to feel validated and finally heard. A good therapist enables you to use your voice and recognize your perception of reality without questioning. It's not easy, as gaslighting does a great job of shaking your sense of security and trust, but most people find the strength to fight with the help of friends and sometimes with a therapist who gets it.

Love Bombing: Overwhelmed by Affection

When we start a new relationship, we sometimes experience love bombing. In other words, a person in a relationship with us might be highly affectionate, give all their attention to us, and spend a lot of time, effort, or things on us. Such makes you feel like you are in heaven. But if you think about it, the massive attention could be less sustainable and realistic. Like, there is no way it can be this great! It all means that sometimes, you fall for what can be called love baiting, meaning you're getting too many gifts, constant text messaging, and just feeling like they are really into you. At first, it may seem that the person you are with really cares for you – sending you sweet letters and buying expensive things. Eventually, you catch on to things and see through every sweet gesture. At the beginning of a relationship, as the routine sets in, you may enjoy it and feel over the moon, often asking yourself, how can such a perfect relationship be possible?

Love bombing is all about control and manipulation, not pure love and affection. Usually, the individual doing the love bombing is driven more by the fear of rejection or desire for power than by love. They show you so much love that you feel you should repay them. It feels like they are bounding you, slowly shifting the power balance in the relationship. Amid all that love and care, getting into a situation where your independence is wholly undermined is simple. Their power over you effectively distorts your judgment, and before you know it, you find yourself in a situation where you are no longer in charge of your own life.

It is vital to distinguish between the intensity of love bombing and the soothing temperature of genuine warmth. Here, genuine affection recognizes the relationship's dynamic, leaving space for individuality, growth, and mutual perception. Genuine affection can be defined through caring gestures that are considerate as opposed to mind-blowing acts that are often consistent rather than sporadic. However, the key feature of genuine affection is that the other person's autonomy is respected. As you might already know, the ultimate purpose of genuine affection is not to overwhelm or control but to build a groundwork of mutual respect and trust.

The way to fight against the manipulation of love bombing begins with the intentional setting of healthy boundaries. Boundaries are an invisible line between personal space, values, and emotional well-being. Such is the ability to protect yourself against the act of overabundant affection. Boundaries enable us to control the space of the relationship by not allowing someone to set a tone that seems comfortable only for them. Such are also important through the development of intimacy, the exchange of personal information, and mutual understanding, which occurs naturally and only when both parties want and feel comfortable with it. In addition, clear boundaries set at the beginning show the potential manipulator that their efforts will not take effect, making the love bombing strategy useless.

Pacing the relationship and allowing yourself to step back and consciously think about the motivations and intensity of the effects of how you are treated is so important. It will enable you to think, observe, and listen to your intuition, allowing you to analyze whether a relationship feels and seems right. As it is premised on self-respect and the understanding of self-worth, such introspection and pacing serve as a filter that separates sincere affection from manipulative ways.

The ability to recognize and comprehend love bombing is crucial. It allows you to remain savvy about all the potential risks. It will enable you to evaluate the initial stages of a relationship, weighing affection and fondness against possible insincerities that come with the intent of manipulation. As you comprehend love bombing, setting boundaries and demands becomes easier, helping you proceed at a considerable pace and safe distance.

Noticing and understanding your feelings requires skill and a willingness to be introspective. When you learn to identify and refer to your emotions, you transform from someone who might be easily manipulated into someone who actively shapes their relational reality. This self-awareness empowers you to engage in relationships from a place of strength and clarity rather than vulnerability. By protecting yourself from the intense and often deceptive tactics of love bombing, you ensure that future relationships are based on genuine affection and mutual respect. This foundation is crucial for fostering relationships that are healthy and capable of growth. Protecting your heart while staying open to genuine connections is one of life's most significant challenges. Balancing these two aspects is incredibly meaningful. In order to achieve this, it's important to focus on the positive elements of relationships while also recognizing their potential pitfalls.

For instance, being aware of love bombing is a crucial tool. It helps you evaluate situations more accurately. By understanding that excessive flattery and affection can be manipulative, you can set boundaries and recognize that such behavior isn't part of a healthy relationship. This awareness allows you to build relationships based on mutual respect and shared experiences, free from control and manipulation. Connecting with others is essential, so learning how to spot manipulative tactics is crucial. This knowledge helps you protect yourself and nurture stronger, more authentic relationships.

The Narcissist's Playbook: Identifying Covert Tactics

As relationships develop, dealing with narcissism can be particularly challenging, especially when it's not easily recognized. Narcissists often come across as insensitive and full of self-importance. Their lives seem like a strategic plan designed to attack others and protect themselves from even the smallest grievances. There are two main types of narcissism: overt and covert. Overt narcissists are easier to spot because they display their arrogance, selfishness, and self-absorption openly.

On the other hand, covert narcissists are more challenging to identify. They hide their narcissistic tendencies behind a facade of vulnerability and admirable personal qualities. Such personalities raid everything they touch. To this day, many studies have been done on how these personalities affect those around them. A study on this found the emotional issues that stem from being around these individuals, specifically when these individuals may be family members, parents, or partners (Nugget, 2023).

Understanding these distinctions can help you navigate relationships more effectively, recognize the signs of narcissism, and protect yourself from potential harm. Narcissistic patterns include a lack of empathy, a strong sense of entitlement, and the exploitation of others, creating a dynamic that can be very damaging. A lack of empathy means that a narcissist can easily ignore other people's feelings and suffering. They usually don't recognize or appreciate their partner's needs, leading to consistently one-sided exchanges where they don't want to treat others with the same consideration they expect. Their sense of entitlement gives them a feeling of immense superiority, which, combined with their exploitative behavior, often disregards the interests and rights of others.

As you interact with new people or stay connected with past acquaintances, being able to distinguish between overt and covert narcissism is crucial. Covert narcissists may appear fragile, hesitant, shy, or even self-deprecating, often radiating a charm that draws others in and elicits support and sympathy. However, despite their outward appearance, they can be just as selfish and manipulative as overt narcissists. Understanding the lengths a narcissist will go to preserve their control and manipulative influence is essential for addressing these issues. This knowledge equips you to protect yourself better and foster healthier, more balanced relationships.

For example, often used and vastly efficient means of manipulation can be seen in the act of triangulation and projection, which are tools that should be recognized to reduce their efficiency. In the case of triangulation, narcissistic individuals pull others into discussions and debates, making the partner feel as if they were comparing themselves to the third party. Such acts can often cause jealousy and the "want" to win their partner's attention, which empowers the narcissist. Projection, on the other hand, allows the narcissist to attribute their behaviors to others through the deflection of blame, avoidance, and responsibility, making others feel like the source of the problem.

You must ensure your boundaries are in place to prevent yourself from falling into these traps. Boundaries and self-esteem represent a powerful defense mechanism, outlining the extent to which the activities and statements in a relationship can occur. By setting your boundaries unromantically and maintaining strict adherence to them, you can protect yourself from the gradually intensified manipulations and control issues that a narcissist uses to elicit a specific response. Although imposing boundaries and maintaining them may seem impossible to use through the conditions of a severe narcissist, the practice is necessary to prevent your loss of self-identity.

Let's keep it accurate. Sometimes, the line between vulnerability and manipulation can be incredibly blurry. That's why the ability to discern genuine sensitivity from covert narcissism is priceless. It gives you the tools to shield yourself from the subtle erosion of self-worth often accompanying such relationships. Instead, it empowers you to seek connections built on mutual respect, empathy, and genuine care. Understanding narcissism and its various forms becomes more than just a defensive strategy—it becomes a proactive pursuit of healthier, more fulfilling relationships. Love and connection can genuinely thrive when equity and respect form the foundation.

This shift in perspective allows you to foster relationships that are not only strong but also profoundly nourishing for both parties involved.

The Highly Sensitive Person's Way of Dealing with Toxic People: Coping Strategies

Our connections and exchanges with others can affect our emotional well-being more than you can imagine. An Individual characterized as a Highly Sensitive Person (HSP) can go beyond his or her feelings by having more empathy and appreciation for the world. While openness heightens their experience and enriches perceptions, it leaves these individuals particularly susceptible to the ravages of abrasive personalities. The emotional damage within specific encounters can be painful and confusing, as emotions can easily be heightened. Sometimes, we go through life without taking a second to analyze ourselves. Take the time to dive into how everyday interactions make you feel. Knowing the nature of your sensitivity is extremely important as you learn to acknowledge your emotions. It allows you to come prepared with the power of awareness and principles designed to shield and support your soul.

The first step that a HSP should undertake to accept sensitivity is to begin by recognizing his or her intrinsic value. It would not simply be the acceptance of their trait but the extent to which it defines their interactions with others. Highly sensitive individuals tend to feel the pressure of their sympathy towards those with a hostile demeanor, as they are more impacted by negativity than the average person. As you pause and analyze your emotions, you can view your situation and ask questions to form a new perspective. HSPs could perceive their sensitivity in a new light as a form of insight that appears when analyzing human behavior in a new way.

An empowered mindset is based on the realization that the depth of emotional experience does not imply vulnerability but rather presents a unique standpoint to which the dynamics of toxicity become evident.

Practically, this means that, from subtle manipulation to a brutal criticism, the HSP does not recognize the unhealthy behavior as a litmus test of their inadequacy but as a mirror of the toxic individual's issues. This realization is crucial because it makes every encounter with toxic individuals not an exhausting emotional flood but an opportunity for establishing boundaries and a chance to speak up.

The HSP's boundary-setting amounts to self-preservation, ensuring that emotional well-being is kept intact in the face of toxicity. These boundaries allow you to interact with others on your terms, whether physical or emotional. It could limit contact with those whose sole purpose is to drain the HSP's reservoir of emotional energy and limit proximity with those who degrade their sensitivity or try to take advantage of it. Still, the main challenge of the process is not in drawing the boundaries but in ensuring they are maintained. Such is a balancing act that is always at risk of tipping. The driving force behind the need for sensitivity is the need to construct nurturing environments and experiences.

On a physical level, HSPs construct their safe space from the world in their surroundings – be it living spaces or openness with others who share and respect their sensitivity, acting as the support network to keep the worst toxic interaction at bay. On an emotional level, it implies nurturing support in the form of hobbies and activities, which replenish their stores of emotional energy – painting, musical composition, or simply long walks in nature to reconnect with the rhythm of their hearts in peace.

Overcoming toxicity is more profound than abiding by establishing boundaries and changing your environment. First and foremost, it is a way of reclamation. To be more exact, it is how a compassionate person reclaims their right to experience the world in their way rather than in a miserable encounter. The point is that by knowing how a harmful and toxic person can be spotted, they can look beyond the line of even deciding to build a relationship with that person. In other words, you can learn to keep them at a distance when you can spot toxic traits. When HSPs can sport this trait, they can internalize and think of a way to explore why certain things happen the way they do and find a reasonable way to overcome them. Afterward, the best thing they can do for themselves is set time aside to reenergize and regain their power from such encounters. Solitude and time away help in a magical way, where people can have time to think of how specific scenarios can be avoided in the future.

As you reenergize, it is also essential to cultivate resilience. As you embrace your power, it should be emphasized that it is indispensable to find the strength to go through all the peculiar features of the nuanced period of the relationship with a toxic person. It needs no heart solidification but a more profound understanding. Though sensitivity makes the HSP the prey for emotions and heightened experiences, it also gives them the intellectual ability to understand their feelings better. It is this unique feature of character that marks their capacity to understand the situation better. They raise empathy toward mindfulness of the encountered issue and, consequently, better overcome it.

Being better connected to one's emotions gives profound insight. It enables the HSP to gain a rich understanding of themselves and the dynamics of toxicity. It provides them a sense of purpose and protection when moving through the world. Their sensitivity is not a burden but the hope that leads them toward connections that honor the depth of their emotional landscape.

Boundary Violations: The Invisible Line

As we explore various human relationships, boundaries serve as threads, marking our personal space and distinguishing each tie from the other. On an emotional, physical, and mental level, these threads delineate our sanity that enables our safeguarding. Although not visible, these boundaries are as accurate as the walls of a fortress, established not for isolation but rather to protect the richness of our inner self from disregard, disrespect, or intrusion. Yet, like all fences, these too are put to the test in their violation—the crossing of the line, either with intent or inadvertently. Crossing the line is as simple as offering unsolicited advice, speaking too closely, or powerfully ignoring a 'no.' Although innocuous in itself, these actions cumulatively exert a sense of control, dominance, or even disregard for the well-being of others.

The tool with which to redraw the line firmly is assertiveness. Communicating boundaries is not necessarily an act of aggression but rather a means of defending your relational space. Such requires a firm message, precise delivery, no apology, and excluding vague language. Effectively, this serves to delineate the rights and boundaries of a relationship. Yet, the most pertaining reason for assertiveness is its ability to convey to the individual their rights in light of the violation. Through assertiveness, line trespassers communicate their awareness of the transgression and the importance of preserving boundaries. Thus, in doing so, assertiveness becomes a tool of protection and a way to protect your self-worth.

The strategy for dealing with those who violate the prescribed boundaries should be firm yet flexible. Consistency in enforcing the boundary is critical, leading to every violation having a response indicating that the other person's proximity is not welcome. Sometimes, the violations persist, suggesting that those who hurt us have inadequate respect for personal boundaries. In such a case, the readiness to leave might be the critical aspect of self-preservation. Despite being emotionally challenging, this choice underlines that the attitude to one's boundary indicates how the other person perceives them. In this regard, the absence of respect for our autonomy should signify that person's attitude toward us.

As you think through past interactions, at some point in our lives, we have had the chance to experience how boundaries can affect the outcome of a particular situation. Think about how empowered that made you feel, even if it was insignificant. That thought should lead you to believe that maintaining personal boundaries is one of the most crucial aspects of human interaction. The invisible lines between the individual and those around them, defined in the realms of the emotional, physical, and mental spaces, encourage us by being and thriving. Boundaries demonstrate respect for yourself, the assignation of value, and the right to privacy and independence.

Human interaction is a careful balance between a drive toward intimacy and a necessity for security, with boundaries bridging the two. For this very reason, boundaries are crucial to protecting ourselves from others. Our intentions serve as the path that will guide us in ensuring that every step toward relationship-building honors the importance of our emotions and personal space.

Emotional Blackmail: The Unsaid Threats

Emotional blackmail occurs in the shadows of human interactions, where the currency is guilt, fear, and obligation. This black market is subtle, as it feeds not on money and material goods but takes advantage of the relationship that two people share to exert power and control. At its core, blackmail is a two-stepped manipulative dance, with one of the two partners leading through the verbal or unspoken threat and the other complying, following their lead but eternally hesitating, driven by fear of losing the relationship or desire to restore harmony.

As you shape and develop relationships, it's easy to find yourself in various forms of emotional abuse, with one of the most common being the threat to end the relationship. Dissatisfaction with the relationship is often seen as a constant issue, making it an efficient act of manipulation. Such discontent usually calls for the loved one's cooperation, where tiny changes are made. These small and subtle changes eventually fall into the loved one's full cooperation. Another common form takes place when affection is not given. Where they stop talking to you and limit their contact, not as a genuine act but rather as a way to manipulate you. Such actions often lead to the manipulator making others feel it's not their fault. All situations usually come down to a single point, which leads to creating relationships in which the blackmailed victim feels an eternal indebtedness and is not in control of their actions but mandated to have their needs and wants in favor of the needs of the blackmailer.

The difficulty with this type of manipulation is that it tends to go unnoticed, with the signs mistaken for ordinary relationship dynamics. The first step towards freeing yourself of the nexus of emotional blackmail is recognizing the blackmail itself and becoming aware of the mechanisms involved. When fully mindful of interactions involving blackmailing, you can also begin to notice the act of compliance within the relationship.

Avoiding emotional blackmail is something that seems difficult but not unfeasible. It all starts with creating an emotional distance – not physical, but the one that makes a gap between yourself and the blackmailer. Mentally backing off is also an explicit, internal way of keeping one's emotional well-being safe and away from the blackmailer's reach. It requires acknowledging that the blackmailer's tactics are just that – manipulation coupled with ingenuity. Knowing this should further enable you to understand how emotional independence should be upheld.

As you navigate through this situation and realize that you are genuinely being blackmailed, know that there is support out there. Working on yourself, along with receiving help, has to be a priority. To maintain the boundaries and restore one's independence, one must resist the situation that has taken shape and not engage in the blackmailer's game. Resisting the blackmailer's tactics is so important, and they can be done by sticking to a rational, correct line – do not allow shifting the dialogue to constructive communication – and sticking to the set boundaries. The blackmailer might "not understand" and "not accept" it initially; nevertheless, sticking to your stance will eventually force them to fail their manipulation. As complying brings the blackmailer "at home" and dissolves the situation, it is also worth being upfront. As you become firm in your stance, you can use the prompt: "Yes, I know that you will be upset, but ..." The steps to resist emotional blackmail involve the following:

- Develop tactics that protect your interests.

- Adjusting to reason.

- Neutralizing the manipulation of the blackmailer in the long run.

As you overcome the threshold of emotional blackmail, you will grow and become a whole different person. This emotional turmoil will make you more robust and fortified against future manipulation attempts. Your life will become living proof, and whether you believe it or not, you might serve as an example to other victims trapped in the cycle of blackmail.

Isolation Tactics: Cutting Off Your Support System

In the struggle for control, isolation becomes the best tool to remove you from your world and those who care about you. It is also a way to ensure submissiveness and time for them. It may begin with your partner making small comments about your friends or family, which may not sit right with you. At first, you brush them off, but they start to eat away at your connections. You often feel that if those friends or family members aren't liked, you shouldn't bring them around or spend time with them. Before you know it, you feel like you're all alone, without the support you used to rely on.

The journey from those initial moments to feeling completely alone happens because of a constant stream of minor manipulations. It makes you feel like each little jab or criticism comes from a caring place, but it pushes you further into isolation. Each comment has one goal – introducing a seed of doubt in the victim's mind concerning their relationships beyond the manipulator. Over time, these small doubts and criticisms can grow into a dense forest of loneliness and reliance, trapping the victim and pulling them away from their support network towards the manipulator.

The re-establishment of isolation is worsened through the bridges you've burned. During these times, the human need for connection cultivates a desire to feel connected to someone who understands you. Escaping the cycle of isolation requires acknowledgment and the need to reestablish burnt bridges. Reaching out to those once close to you is the first step. Doing so can make you feel embarrassed or scared because this situation might also make you feel like a horrible friend, colleague, or family member. These actions, however, become a crucial moment. You may slowly reestablish your connection if you don't witness rejection from those you've shunned. Don't think of them as bad friends if you are rejected, but rather understand that you have also prioritized the manipulator unintentionally due to being a victim of their subtle tactics. Tactics that have pulled you away from connecting to others.

The reopening of burnt bridges is as much about reconnecting lost contacts as it is about making new ones. Dueling clubs, counseling appointments, and community-building opportunities provide spaces where victims can re-socialize, create support, and build spaces for validation. These new connections, built on the foundation of shared suffering and support, create mental armor against the perpetrator's victimization, offering tools to escape isolation.

Thus, reconnection, while essential to shattering the chains of the isolator's control, is also a reaffirmation that you are strong enough. Such is a statement of your independence and a way to move toward reclaiming your right to relationship building. In such doing, there is a resurrection of the self; it allows you to regain the power and self-determination blotted out by the cohorts of isolation and manipulation. Finding your way from isolation to reconnection is a fantastic feeling, a metamorphosis process casting off the veils of dependence and insecurity to reveal a core of strength and self-assuredness. This process, filled with moments of skepticism and victory, is ultimately not about rebuilding lost connections but redefining the self about others. Restructuring the social cloth that balances individual self-reliance, respect for the autonomy of others, and the human aptitude for empathy.

Feeling alone amid all the complicated relationships we encounter is like a wake-up call on power dynamics. Such dynamics are critical in how we interact with each other. It's a reminder to pay attention to how we see 'power' and 'control' in our connections. It's also a chance to start fresh—to figure out what relationships mean to you and how to build better support networks.

The Cycle of Abuse: Recognizing the Patterns

Toxic relationships often feel like a twisted dance - both familiar and suffocating. They create a harmful cycle that, while predictable, inflicts deep wounds. If we examine this cycle closely, it's clear it's not just a series of isolated incidents. It's a dark, ongoing pattern that traps the victim. Each phase of this cycle - from tension building to explosion to reconciliation and back - plays a crucial role. In the tension-building phase, things may start small, but the tension keeps growing, making the victim feel like they're walking on eggshells, waiting for something to snap.

After a traumatic event, the reconciliation phase can seem like a ray of hope after the darkness. The abuser might apologize, give gifts, and promise to change, making the victim believe things will get better. It's like a temporary relief, a chance to think that tomorrow will be different. But this hope doesn't last long. Soon, there's a calm period - a deceptive quiet before the storm. Everything feels settled but sometimes plans for more violence could be brewing underneath the surface. This calmness tricks the victim into feeling safe again. It's a time for reflection, but it's short-lived. Suddenly, the cycle repeats with another outburst of manipulations to the possible act of violence. Each phase chips away at the victim's confidence and hope for escape. Breaking free from this cycle isn't easy, but there are ways forward, which I'll discuss in the following sections.

Recognition alone may not be adequate to escape; thus, external interventions are essential to provide the needed support and resources to escape the cycle. Through support systems, you can receive practical support and guidance, including the validation that the experiences you are going through are not typical. Emotional blackmail and promises play a significant role in drawing you back to the abuser, who may hope for a better outcome, which in turn also gives you hope for change. Manipulation, however, is not the only factor; other psychological aspects, such as guilt, fear, and obligation, also play a significant role in drawing you back to the abuser.

Even if you feel stuck in an abusive cycle with no way out, remember there's always hope. It's tough to rebuild your sense of control, self-worth, and a journey of strength and progress. It's about confronting the tough times and finding the courage to build a brighter future for yourself.

Triangulation: When Three's a Crowd

Among the intricate relations of humans, triangulation emerges as one of the key tactics, a subtle but impactful manipulation tool. These chess moves of 'emotional chess' imply deploying elements of relationships alongside a third party to formulate the complex transformation of the interaction between two people. As such, a steering hand manipulates the perspectives, views, or very presence of a third party to achieve the destabilization of their partner, shading the pictures with doubts and sensations of isolation. The most striking examples of triangulation are conversational tactics, where a third party's opinion or action is presented to the other partner to discard their views or decisions. It might be a dinner table, where a partner's choices are somewhat criticized in light of another's wishes or a disagreement that is warmly greeted by an outsider's point of view, making the partner not just the opposite but separated.

Though they seem like mere discourses, the instances above are about control, the subtle silencing of their partner to strengthen the voice of a third party further. The aura of triangulation, in turn, results in another form of manipulation, where the weaker partner should doubt the integrity of their union. They've felt secure about their relationship, a shared experience cultivated with trust, intimacy, and passion, but now they are their bond's ground with another human. It's the fabrication of a feeling that the third party's presence is in the room; the couple's privacy is only a convenient concept that can be breached when it becomes necessary for one of the partners. In the new shared space, this feeling grows with each new triangulation, the flora of doubts growing into a lonely castle of isolation.

Resisting manipulation demands assertiveness—a steadfast refusal to entertain outside interference in matters that belong solely to you and your partner. It's about communicating directly and clearly, especially when confronting manipulative behavior. By clarifying boundaries and standing united as a couple, you reclaim your autonomy and strengthen your bond. This firm stance disrupts the manipulator's tactics and reaffirms the importance of your relationship. Together, you assert your independence and protect the integrity of your partnership against any further attempts to undermine it.

Choosing not to engage in discussions involving third parties isn't a retreat; it's a stance of strength. By refusing to play into the manipulator's game, we safeguard our relationships from the chaos of triangulation. Though setting this boundary can be challenging, it's vital for preserving the integrity of our connection. It's a declaration of our agency, signaling our commitment to steering the relationship away from manipulation and conflict. This decision isn't about weakness; it's about empowerment. It's the moment we seize control of our relationship's course, steering it away from the edge where the manipulator wants us to stumble. By sidestepping the pitfalls of triangulation, we chart a hopeful path forward—a path worth navigating despite its challenges.

Unwritten social norms and relationships often dictate our interactions; it's essential to approach seemingly peaceful situations with a hint of caution. Triangulation, a subtle form of manipulation, can quietly seep into these connections, damaging trust and intimacy. To combat this toxicity, we must regain control of our communication channels and preserve the authenticity of our connections. It's not just about fulfilling a promise; it's about building relationships based on honesty and open dialogue. Choosing against manipulation isn't just a duty; it's about nurturing relationships grounded in trust and transparency.

There are countless ways partners can respond to challenges like triangulation. However, addressing this issue as soon as it is presented is often seen as a necessary step—a promise made by those involved in the relationship. Squashing this behavior serves a dual purpose: it shields the ties from the harmful effects of triangulation and reinforces its foundation of honesty and open communication. This commitment catalyzes the relationship, empowering it to avoid any potential harm.

CHAPTER 2

NAVIGATING THE MAZE: UNDERSTANDING AND OVERCOMING THE IMPACT OF TOXIC RELATIONSHIPS

A fter a period of chaos, people can sometimes develop a unique and strong connection, quietly drawing them closer together. This connection is not based on love but on shared pain, and it can keep individuals tied to those who've hurt them deeply. This strange paradox makes us rethink what it means to connect with others and be resilient, pushing us to explore and understand its nuances.

Understanding the Trauma Bond

Since the 1970s, psychologists have been exploring the concept of 'trauma bonding,' which describes the complex emotional ties that develop between someone who's suffered and the person who caused that suffering. It's like the bond that can form between hostages and their captors, but it happens in relationships that are supposed to be close. This bond isn't based on genuine love or loyalty but rather on a mix of abuse and occasional kindness that creates a solid emotional connection.

Characteristics of Trauma Bonds

Trauma bonds are complex. Victims often feel torn between their loyalty to their abusers and the abuse they endure. It's not just about defending the abuser or thinking the abuse is okay. Sometimes, it's about feeling strangely tied to them. This loyalty isn't because the abuser has good qualities; it's more like a way for victims to cope with what's happening, even if it doesn't make sense. The confusion comes from the rollercoaster of emotions – one moment, there's cruelty, the next, kindness. It creates this hope that things will improve, even though the victim knows it's not right.

Breaking the Bond

Going through this painful journey is not easy. I hope that you find the strength to let go of the trauma bond. It can be rather challenging, and it may seem never to end. Instead of pushing hard, those going through this must begin with smaller steps. Seeking help from a therapist can make a big difference, as they will provide the necessary tools to understand your trauma. They are the guiding light in this intricate, profound, and challenging process.

Healing Process

Healing from trauma bonds isn't a straightforward journey. There may be a lot of setbacks alongside breakthroughs. There is no need to give up yourself due to the slow progress because it takes time. You can compare overcoming a trauma bond with healing physical wounds. Sometimes, a broken bone needs time to heal, and so does your mind. It requires some amount of time to rest after a traumatic experience. The truth is, there is no way to rush through this process, and the only thing you can do is create an appropriate environment to keep going forward.

Reflection Section: Identifying Your Bond

A series of journal prompts invites you to reflect on your relationship, helping you recognize any signs of a trauma bond:

- As you recall moments of kindness, are you finding yourself defending your abuser?

- Document these instances and the reasons you provided. Some may include your challenges in life, personal stress, upbringing, or other arguments.

- What are you feeling when you are separated or away? Be honest. Are you feeling a sense of relief, anxiety, loss, or a combination of different emotions?

- List the reasons for staying. Do they include hope for change, reluctance to be alone, or a dependent financial situation?

These prompts are designed for you to review constantly, offering you a mirror in your evolving understanding of the dynamics in your relationships.

Resource List: Support for Breaking Trauma Bonds

Practical support is provided through a curated list of resources, including hotlines, support groups, and recommended readings. This list serves as a bridge, connecting individuals with communities and information to help them walk away from toxic relationships and towards recovery. In the maze of a toxic relationship, figuring out the concept of trauma bonding is like finding a hidden key. It allows you to see why seemingly inexplicable loyalty and attachment to an abuser and the painful understanding of it is the essential first step out of the shadows of manipulation and into the light of self-recovery.

The Long Shadow: PTSD from Toxic Relationships

After you leave that toxic relationship, the touch of a fallout can haunt you like a shadow that stalks you consistently. It may not be something vivid to your eyes, but it's stuck so deep within you. It is so much that it has long-lasting cuts on your heart and mind. That kind of shadow is referred to as Post-Traumatic Stress Disorder or PTSD by experts, and it is not only limited to soldiers. It happens to anyone after an emotional and traumatic experience. Living with PTSD is like finding yourself locked in a maze of some kind. Every day is challenging, and you have to attribute it to some occasional habits, such as feeling uneasy all the time and having scary nightmares and flashbacks. These are not just some pains of the past; they are tangible demons affecting your life.

PTSD can be annoying, especially if you're not sure of the way out. Treating it by all means possible is the best thing you can do for yourself. Seeking help is doable, and therapy can genuinely help. It enables you to manage your PTSD through intimate study or various modes of treatment. One of the most popular treatments is called cognitive-behavioral therapy (CBT), which helps you and your therapist grasp and change the thoughts and behaviors caused by PTSD. Logically, rebuilding after trauma is a lengthy process.

Along with receiving help from your therapist, medications can also help reduce some of the symptoms of PTSD. As you focus on the moment and practice mindfulness, you can also help yourself by letting go of the past. Grounding techniques enable you not to let the past drag you down. You can train your senses through grounding to help you return to reality when you feel like disappearing. If you're feeling better, you can ask your therapist to introduce you to group therapy. Within, you can find other survivors and be inspired by them. Being around people who understand what you're going through can be helpful. Sometimes it's just nice to know you were not the only person in this crappy situation.

As you decide whether therapy is right for you, you must remember that exploring PTSD after leaving a toxic relationship is a challenging journey. It's your chance to show how tough and badass you are. A storm can be hard to overcome, but there is always a shining dawn. With support and proper guidance, you won't have to die in a storm but walk through it towards the rainbow.

Self-Esteem and Self-Worth: The Invisible Wounds

Our self-esteem can be shattered while in a toxic relationship, fading away like metal rusting in the rain. The constant neglect and belittling take away our confidence and destroy our self-love, hurting us through an invisible wound. Similarly, and in many cases, as we interact with people in a toxic manner, we also learn to build a coping mechanism that begins to diminish others around us. In light of this, self-esteem and its reclamation are not merely a single activity but a healing process through small steps.

In the first stage, this invisible wound can be healed with affirmations seen as a verbal and mental ointment. From the first days of their application, they work as a counter-narrative to one you have accepted and internalized. It may seem a simple tool, but it is powerful in its effects, which have been proven for centuries. Day after day, as you repeat their aspirations to yourself, you construct a new narrative about yourself. You can use every word as a brick to build a new self.

As mentioned, therapy is another interventional tool people use to rediscover themselves. In the therapeutic context, you can excavate yourself layer by layer, knowing that there is a preventive barrier between your initial self and the perception that toxic relationships have created. These layers not only hide wounds but, as the therapist (your excavation helper), guide you to see the potential of the person within you. In such a way, the interaction with the therapist helps transform the tainted self-esteem into self-awareness.

A critical step in recovering self-esteem involves distinguishing between self-worth and external validation. This distinction is frequently blurred in toxic relationships. Victims of such connections become dependent on the appraisal of abuse, and their value becomes tied to that unstable foundation. Therefore, finding their true self-worth involves a strategic change of perspective, from seeking others' acknowledgment to feeling validated within. An apt description of this contrast is seeking nourishment from ominous mirages to tapping into the pure well of self-worth.

Another crucial factor for this foundation is a balanced environment. Social connections support your values and provide a reinforcing shield against outside negativity. Such networks reflect and create the individuals' sense of worth, becoming a source of collective acknowledgment. This reflection is crucial for victims stuck in toxic relationships. By seeing yourself not through the eyes of others but through the mirror of support, individuals become validated, and others reaffirm their worth.

Case Studies of Reclaimed Self-Esteem

A series of case studies effectively demonstrates the multidimensional aspects of overcoming a toxic relationship and restoring self-esteem. These stories differ in characteristics and peculiarities but are united by the theme of their transformation with the help of self-discovery, therapy, and support from the surrounding community. They depict the experiences of different people who succeeded in going through the challenges and joys of toxic and other kinds of relationships and promote a variety of stories showing the way to restoring the perception of the self from a person with wholly ruined self-esteem to the one who is confident about the value and usefulness of their personality. The path from rock bottom and accepting your life as worthless to the top of self-awareness and acceptance is guided by the processes of self-improvement. Through support and finding a professional who can help you deal productively with the new life, you have the chance to overcome toxic relationships.

Anxiety and Depression: The Emotional Aftermath

Toxic entanglements never go without a trace; they tend to leave a trace where anxiety or depression (or both) become the reflection of such relationships. Often, being a pain is deep within us, a pain that never goes away, almost like a never-ending song of suffering echoing deep. Depression is like a heavy cloak that wraps around our weary spirit, drowning it in darkness and dampness, extinguishing any flicker of hope or joy. While anxiety and depression might seem like separate struggles, they're just two sides of the same coin – both are often born from toxic relationships.

Common Outcomes

The development of anxiety and depression after toxic relations is not accidental. These psychological disorders appear because of the extreme and prolonged pressure on people. Such leads to a significant decrease in self-esteem and constant hyperarousal of the organism. Anxiety is characterized by severe feelings of anxiety that accompany people 24 hours a day and in any situation. Depression is associated with feelings of exhaustion and permanent despair that cover the world with grey colors. It is how a human being is doomed to exist in the shadow of the past for a significant period.

Symptom Management

As you navigate through your symptoms, such has to call for a flexible approach, usually leaning on both therapy and medication as the main pillars of support. As previously discussed, having the will to get better and seek help is the most crucial part of your journey towards healing. Therapy acts as that initial guiding light, diving deep into our inner conflicts with empathy, helping us understand ourselves better. Along with treatment, other supportive measures can come into play, like medication or additional therapies, to help you through this psychological journey. And lastly, making lifestyle changes—like exercising, getting enough sleep, and eating well—can also play a significant role in the recovery process.

Understanding Triggers

One of the critical elements of this journey is identifying your triggers, those seemingly harmless things that evoke feelings of depression and anxiety. It is the equivalent of understanding the minefield of your mind so that you may avoid it or dismantle it when it appears. This identification process is a concern that requires an honest and gentle reflection of your life, recognizing that every trigger is a sign hovering above the road. It is thought to understand that a part of our soul can remain in the past, struggling with the traumas we have experienced. We can overcome our triggers by gaining the proper knowledge and understanding of what triggers us.

Seeking Support

Yes, I will reemphasize support! Believe it or not, this cannot be overstated. These networks become a lifeline that teaches you how to reflect and do so healthier by delving into positivity, worth, and understanding. There lies reward in the arms of these networks, shared strength, and collective wisdom. It is here where therapeutic intervention, community support, and personal strength meet, where anxiety and depression begin to heal. It is a long, winding road marked with victories and losses, yet with each passing one of these, there is a reminder that recovery is repeatedly achievable and proven.

Breaking Free from Victim Mentality

After toxic relationships end, a sense of powerlessness remains in most cases—the feeling subdues your wants and messes with reality, often leading to a victim cycle. Every newly created dynamic is seen through your need to protect your integrity against outside threats. It's easy to become passive and lenient, letting your persistence fade into resignation. This feeling creates a swirling cycle, where you wait for circumstances to overpower you like chains still holding onto the remnants of past experiences.

Identifying the Victim Mentality

The first step to breaking out of the cycle is identifying the habitual patterns that support it. In most cases, several behavior habits form the totality of background support of the cycle. The behavior I have identified is the introduction of multiple self-fulfilling prophecies – constant hypervigilance and a state of defense that one enters upon interacting with most people. The world is always against you as if you have no control over your emotions. There are always "buts" and "however," endless complaints and a tendency to blame everything and everyone else. Recognizing these patterns takes soul-searching and a willingness to dig deep into your life story.

Empowerment Strategies

Shifting from a victim mentality to an empowerment mentality is like flipping a switch inside yourself. It's all about going from feeling helpless and controlled by circumstances to taking charge of your life. This transformation doesn't happen overnight – it's a significant change that requires a shift in how you approach things. First, you must realize that you control your happiness, decisions, and actions. No one else can make those choices for you. Next, instead of dwelling on problems, focus on finding solutions and alternatives. Look at what you can change or influence, and tackle those aspects head-on. Finally, align your actions with your goals and values. By digging deep into your strengths and finding ways to tackle challenges head-on, you turn obstacles into opportunities for growth and learning. It's about taking ownership of your life and making the most of every situation, no matter how tough it may seem.

Role of Therapy

In the journey from feeling like a victim to embracing a survivor mindset, therapy becomes your guide, leading you through past traumas toward a future filled with strength and self-determination. In treatment, you start digging into the roots of your victim mentality, understanding how experiences of disempowerment and loss of control shaped your view of yourself. It's a safe space where you're encouraged to rewrite your story, emphasizing your resilience instead of your past struggles.

Therapists use techniques to help you become more self-aware, challenge negative beliefs, and strengthen your ability to stand up for yourself. It's all about letting go of old patterns and building new ones that empower you to see yourself in a new light. Taking time to acknowledge and celebrate your progress along the way is crucial. By celebrating these victories, you're rewriting your narrative, shifting from a story of victimhood to one of resilience and empowerment.

Moving away from the shadow of victim mentality is a profound transformation. It's about reclaiming your agency and challenging the toxic beliefs that once held you back. You'll experience highs and lows, obstacles and victories along the way, but with each step forward, you shed more of the old baggage, revealing a landscape where you control your destiny. In this new journey, you're not defined by your past – you're empowered by it, which gives you the chance to face your destiny on your terms.

The Role of Cognitive Dissonance in Attachment

While it is likely to experience the strongest emotions, love plays a central role in human life. It allows the development of intimate connections and bonds to help people navigate challenging times. This complex emotion, however, can come with its issues. It often involves a convoluted matrix of other human emotions and attachments where love and cognitive dissonance are usually inextricably connected. In attachment, cognitive dissonance can be defined as the discomfort created by holding two conflicting beliefs simultaneously.

In the framework of a toxic relationship, cognitive dissonance reveals the gap between the need for affection and crediting others for having positive traits and behavior. As a result, the dissonance fueled by the abuser's manipulative behavior and corresponding justification on the part of the victim stops them from leaving the relationship. As such, cognitive dissonance and attachment can be seen as two processes that fuel a vicious cycle, making it impossible for the victim to leave an abusive relationship.

When the abuser hits a rough patch, it's like being caught in a tug-of-war. On one side, the victim's behavior might get more intense, especially when they're dealing with job loss or other stresses. But then, every once in a while, the abuser does something unexpectedly kind, shining a light on a different side of them. These moments make it hard for the victim to walk away entirely as they still see glimmers of hope in the relationship. So, such instances can often not make situations as clear-cut as they should be. It's not just good or bad. It's a messy mix of both, leaving many confused and conflicted. However, recognizing this complexity is an important step. It's about acknowledging that things aren't always black and white and learning to navigate the gray areas. It's a reminder to stay aware of the conflicting feelings and guard against falling into the trap of cognitive dissonance in the future.

Therapeutic methods developed to resolve cognitive dissonance in the case of toxic attachments offer a glimmer of hope, providing a way to reconcile the feelings of ambivalence. In this context, treatment acts as a tour guide. It assists a person in finding the best way to navigate the sea of internal discord. Specifically, via tools that encourage reflection, therapists urge their patients to review the ideas and concepts that allow them to perceive and stay connected to the abuser. By doing so, they create opportunities for identifying the process of rationalization that the affected person uses as a coping mechanism. Such allows them to build new beliefs based on the patient's understanding and expectations from relationships.

Internal rationalization is another premise on which the process of cognitive reinforcement can be based. It allows us to question the relationship and question our own beliefs. When your beliefs are reinforced, it's not about forcing you to think a certain way. It's more about validating what you already believe about yourself. With support and understanding, you can start to feel confident and sure of yourself. It's essential to recognize that these reinforcement moments aren't necessarily harmful. They're a necessary part of the healing process. They help you work through your conflicting thoughts and feelings, paving the way for healthier relationships in the future.

The rigidity of cognitive dissonance entwines us in the crawl-like existence of endless undeclared battles. A toxic whirlwind keeps a person rigid, determined, and alert. It taints the internal perception of personal truth with a questionable lens and each step of the dissonance resolution journey where transformation occurs. Reclaiming our identities is a personal journey filled with moments of reconciliation and self-discovery. It's not some dramatic movie scene where everything suddenly clicks into place. Instead, it's like slowly wading into a gentle stream, feeling the soothing flow wash away the chaos of conflicting thoughts and emotions. With each step we take towards finding harmony within ourselves, we're defining the contours of our identity. In these quiet moments of reflection and introspection, we reclaim pieces of who we are. As we do, the turbulent waters of toxic thinking calm, replaced by a sense of peace and serenity.

Life is too short to wait for a big epiphany, and after its immense accomplishment, you may think, now what? What lasts is not a story of clash and indecision; what lasts is regarded as evidence of how you will resolve and sustain your spirit. The path from tangled dissonance to wholesome attachment might be challenging, but it is a road you can define.

Reclaiming Your Identity After Toxicity

Toxic relationships can leave us feeling like we've lost ourselves, like worn-out tapestries with frayed edges from all the rubbing and pulling. It's not just about healing from the damage; it's about rediscovering who we are and stitching back the pieces of our identity. That's where hobbies and fun activities come in. Revisiting the things we used to love before the toxicity took over can help us reconnect with parts of ourselves, we thought were lost. Whether you focus on activities like painting, hiking, or playing music, these activities can offer a path back to your true self. They can help you shake off the effects of toxic relationships and reclaim your identity.

Activities that sustain and recharge individuals become safety havens and a return ticket to themselves. Therefore, playing piano or guitar or putting a brush on canvas or paper in an attempt to resound the painful tune of a toxic relationship is a way to both claim and reclaim the remains of the self. This seemingly small act of defiance serves a larger purpose. It is a way to recover from the trauma of a toxic relationship and reconnect with yourself.

Setting personal goals is another building block in the process of identity rebuilding. Whether modest or grand, these goals create a trajectory of advancement and progress that contrasts the standstill anchored by toxic behavior. They also provide a sense of purpose and a manual for moving through the pains of recovery. Every time a goal is achieved, it is marked as a milestone of growth, which, in turn, cements the sense of agency within the individual and the realization that there is a potential that goes beyond the point of stagnation. Further on, goals allow an individual to reach towards something, thus forming the future that has been robbed initially, thus gradually forming an identity.

The reclamation process falls under attempting self-exploration, a method of excavating your inner self, allowing you to discover your identity. Your likes, dislikes, and values are things to fantasize and dream about. This process deems itself solely reflective and does not exclude sharing within groups or therapy. Groups and therapy function as a mirror where you can see yourself through a collective forum where your experience can be shared. It grants an opportunity to voice your agony.

As you listen to your story through the voice of others, the rediscovery of your identity becomes palpable. Therapy will help you find your identity and lead you through the process. Therapists are not necessarily the architects who help you shape your identity but the choreographers who guide you in finding the person within you.

Independence is like the key that unlocks the door of dependence. It's the starting point, the crucial first step towards breaking free from that vicious cycle. Gaining your independence is practical and psychological. It can be financial independence, the availability of personal space, thoughts, and the ability not to be influenced. Independence is like a rich soil where we plant the seeds of our interests, needs, and values. It's our little nest where we can grow into the person we truly want to be, not what others expect us to be. And it's not just about being on our own – it's about having control over our emotions, motivations, morals, and sense of self. It's like having a shield that protects us from being manipulated by others, giving us the power to stay true to ourselves.

As you build your community and become involved in your growth through psychotherapy, it strengthens your "I." A vast amount of mirrors of groups and the psychotherapeutic alliance will eventually reflect the degree of reclamation. Your recognition will come from pure achievements and regresses, forming the necessary feedback. Role patterns of the collective behavior also "lay the groundwork" as you go through the steps needed to overcome your pain. As you reach the end of the road and discover yourself again, your identity formation will become an entirely new individuality. As our uniqueness has been shaped based on prior experiences, please know that you still have an opportunity to change and grow from everything you've learned. We can only get better! And you are the master of how you want the rest of your life and individuality to be shaped.

Our identity comprises diverse experiences, values, and traits that form a unique picture. But when toxic influences unravel it, it destroys that perfect picture, and putting it back together isn't easy. When our identity is destroyed, it's not just about returning to who we were before but embracing who we are now and who we can become. It's about reclaiming and shaping our identity into something new and empowering.

The Effects of Toxicity in Developing Children

When toxic relationships constantly bombard a child's mind, aggression becomes like a silent storm, leaving behind a trail of chaos. It's hard not to notice the effects of prolonged exposure to toxicity, and aggression can sometimes be a red flag that things have gotten worse. Understanding that aggression isn't just about one person or experience is essential. Toxic relationships come in many forms, and they all have the potential to trigger aggression. These dynamics can contribute to aggressive behavior, whether

constant volatility, manipulation, or neglect. So, when trying to understand where aggression comes from, it's crucial to consider the complexity
of toxic relationships and how they impact everyone involved.

Observing and comprehending the specifics of a child's behavioral or
academic changes is extremely important. In most cases, a child might
become highly aggressive, even towards those who attempt to help them.
Such behavior indicates that the child might not receive the required attention, often resulting in fluctuating academic performance.

While the source of each issue is different, they all point to unhappiness
and turmoil that come as a response to the toxicity they are experiencing.

The first and most crucial issue that you need to understand when
dealing with aggression and toxic relationships is that aggression is not the
cause but the symptom. It is a child's reaction to the surrounding chaos, the
mechanism they adopted to reflect the adults' volatility and uncertainty.
In the context of withdrawal, it constitutes a shield and a closed-off shell
of solitude in which a child hides from the world that proved itself to be
unsafe. In the context of toxic relationships, it is an attempt to find a lasting
solution to the world that has never been safe and to assert some control.

Intervention comes next, and it starts with establishing a secure and
non-toxic environment. The heart of this intervention is honesty and
openness. It's all about laying down the foundation, building a bridge that
helps us understand each other better. It's not just about offering support
and validation but also about being genuine in our intentions. Generally,
a talk should focus on children's emotions and feelings about situations
and the people they are expected to communicate with or live with and
discuss certain vital features or activities. In such a way, the process of
talking becomes the tool for opening some previously closed communication channels due to the atmosphere of fear and suppression, which could
be observed in most families of abusers. They could doubt the worth of
such techniques, and as a typical reaction, they could show that they do
not believe in such intentions of adults who try to talk for the first time,

with inevitable disappointments. Still, even such talks could bring some positive results as they are the starting point for further communication and a preventive step towards further therapeutic actions or personal improvement. For example, one of the ideas in our case is that professional help, be it counseling or some therapeutic approach, could guarantee some level of protection and let abusers find a place to talk in a free and friendly atmosphere. A specific pattern of behavior is typical in such cases. Still, it would be partially broken if this help would be provided with the ability to affect the talk's success. As a preventive measure, the issue of education and emotional literacy could be helpful as a protective tool.

Though its influence upon the developing child is undoubtedly profound, toxicity is by no means a final sentence of all future defined by an emotional and psychological ghost of what should have been a formative period of growth and maturation. Through intervention, the establishment of a safe and supportive environment, open lines of communication, and education in the proactive practice of emotional literacy and the negotiation of interpersonal relationships, a new lease on life, one defined not by victimhood but by personal actualization and healing. From such a starting point, young people can not only come to distinguish toxic relationships and avoid them but also develop a sense of themselves beyond such dynamics, secure in their understanding and appreciation of who they are and how they should interact with others. The developing child, therefore, exists within a nexus of forces and influences that open two distinctive paths, one dispiriting and ghostly, the other hopeful and healing. Ultimately, the role of parent, educator, and mental health professional is not merely to repair the damage wrought by the former but to set the developing child upon the latter through a holistic education based upon care, compassion, and empathy towards the child and their unique path to a sense of self and a healthy way of being in the world.

Surviving vs. Thriving: Changing Your Mindset

Amid the fallout from toxic relationships, there comes a moment when you have to choose between just surviving and truly thriving. In these cases, there appears to exist an entire perspective shift that goes well beyond anything anyone can comprehend when simply enduring abuse or betrayal. Positive thinking, although challenging, can lead to a powerful transformation, creating a sense of 'rebirth' for those who embrace it after tough times. Tendencies, however, can lead to a qualitative shift in relations with the atmosphere and can liberate you from the shackles of prior destructive effects.

The first step in this transformation consists of the survivors' efforts to nurture the positive, thus directing their consciousness onto moments of light piercing through profound memories of darkness. Essentially, the power of instituting positive thinking derives from survivors' inclinations towards the acknowledgment of the present by perceiving it as a solemn reality in the form of their current ability to witness the beauty of the world, the pragmatic nature of human interactions, the grace of love, and other inspiring occurrences. A "growing gratitude" implies a perception of the miraculous, capable of encapsulating the sense of wonder in simple, daily activity. Naturally, such an attitude does not try to counteract the concept of pain a survivor has from their past but instead seeks to serve as a parallel to it. Ways to generate joy do indeed exist.

Supporting positive meaning is the parallel of empowerment from setting and meeting goals. A critical part of the transition from merely surviving to thriving is establishing and pursuing these targets and having them serve as your internal compass. If an individual establishes these goals clearly and shadows them with the sheer force of will, they will function as mile markers of their journey of learning what it truly means to self-actualize. Each goal's completion demonstrates that the individual's destiny is within their control and serves to remind them of their agency, of their power to change reality based on their will. The process of goal-setting and subsequent achievement provides an excellent example of an individual's ability to pick themselves up and keep moving forward, a declaration of their independent strength for all to hear.

A third layer of the concept of thriving is community and connection. After all the anxiety, isolation, and manipulation associated with toxic relationships, the values of humane, genuine connections and the warmth and support they can provide cannot be underestimated. The connection the individual makes with others based on shared experience or some other newfound context provides the psychological nourishment, the sense of belonging, and the support necessary. In addition, one of the crucial functions of such connections is that they reflect self-worth and humanity. Overall, the above-described aspects contribute to the concept of thriving by promoting an individual's connections with their inherent value or ability in case of goals.

If survival is the state of being, then thriving is the philosophy – a mindset with existential and pragmatic connotations. It is not just about recovery from the wounds left by survival; it is about an active, vibrant state of being. Perceivable as the quintessence of the preceding discussions, thriving can be viewed as the inevitable state that an individual experiences when all of the above factors are in place. Rather than the state of being, it can be considered a personal philosophy that not only colors the individual's communication with the world but transforms it completely.

The transition from surviving to thriving is bound to be a rocky one. After all, change is always associated with inner turmoil, fear, and refusal. Nevertheless, the drab cocoon that allowed the individual to survive in the grueling circumstances of the past is finally shed, with no tentative new shell taking its place. Instead, the shining, iridescent wings emerge, and the newfound self takes flight, desperate to explore the world, communicate with others, learn new things, and embrace their passions. Thriving is sure to be a paradise of its own, a personal heaven of rich and fulfilling experiences full of majestic relationships, blissful connections, and the pursuit of knowledge, and thriving is the crown jewel of the experience. The path to thriving is challenging and filled with thorns, but with each successful step, the climber's hand will be enriched with a beautiful rose.

Emotional Depletion: Recharging Your Inner Battery

Following a challenging relationship, there's a profound exhaustion that settles in. It's a fatigue born from navigating toxicity day in and day out that is spent around toxic people. Although intangible, the phenomenon still deserves to be christened with an appropriately heavy name – for example, emotional depletion. It signifies the emptiness of one's reserves and the lack of the whimsical resilience and vitality one gets from living well. Recognition of such a state is highly dependent on how much energy a person puts into monitoring themselves for signs of retreat to start the strenuous journey to recovery and improvement.

Such signs include muted emotions that do not touch the soul or provoke the same kind of joy they once did. It also manifests in the constant feeling of disconnectedness from self and others. One's self shifts into a whisper, and it speaks of a spiritual well that has either dried up or gotten mad. Recognizing the symptoms and the reasons calls for a significant landmark in one's outlook on life. From there, self-care practices become one's lifeblood. They can be as simple as remembering to breathe appropriately and taking moments to feel the pulse of one's body. They can become as involved as rekindling one's dormant hobbies, be it reading, writing, drawing, or creating any other type of art. They signify an act of recovery.

Establishing emotional boundaries is a part of this process, where one decides on one's limits and the extent of the flow of energy and emotion to other people. These boundaries are clear, distinct, and virtually palpable for an external observer; they are guardians of one's vulnerable recovery. With the setting of limits, one perceives which person invests more or less in their established interaction and adjusts the balance. Therefore, with every boundary one set, one creates protection for one's emotional wealth and re-establishes one's respect to be self and recognition of the dirty game intended to bring them out of balance.

At the same time, the activities that arouse feelings of bliss and the most vital interest in one's life contribute to the process and help in recharging one emotionally. This is the pursuit of joy, in which one explores several experiences that leave one scintillating. Whether it is the feeling of bursting into laughter, the satisfaction of reaching a peak in one's career path, or peace provided by a touch of the world's nature, each joyful moment works as healing of all the wounds inflicted by the exhausting, toxic person. They are all pieces of a puzzle of recovery, which are crucial for the big picture of recharging one. The image is not carved in black-and-white colors: it varies in simplicity or complexity, but it always creates a cushion of comfortable content around one, which is the diametric opposite of depressive weariness. Finally, this is not the strategy of escape but rather a confrontation strategy because charging one accumulates more power for facing the toxic remnants of dissipating relationships.

In conclusion, the passage from emotional depletion to the shores of replenishment is a journey that speaks to the resilience of the human condition. It speaks to the ability to climb out of the pits and fill the empty ranks of vitality and joy. A path that includes willful self-care, reclaiming and establishing boundaries, and reclaiming joy echoes the broader timeline of recovery from the fallout of toxic bonds. On the next page, the lessons and advice from this quest and the strategies derived from the crucible of emptiness and revitalization should offer shelter and a guide to safety as you proceed to sail the murky waters of relationships and self-exploration.

CHAPTER 3

Navigating Through Your Recovery with Confidence

A fter going through toxic relationships, you might find your emotional state in a mess, with your self-esteem, confidence, and peace of mind all torn apart by manipulation and neglect. Healing isn't just about returning to how you were before; it's about rebuilding yourself stronger than ever. This chapter will guide you through that journey by showing you practical ways to rebuild yourself from the ground up.

Embracing the Journey: The First Steps to Healing

Taking initial steps is crucial when you're aiming for a specific goal. It allows you to lay the foundation for a journey ahead. With a solid start, it's easier to reach your desired state. Your steps should be considered or practiced carefully and thoughtfully for healing.

As far as the groundwork is concerned, the silence that envelops a person from realizing that something is wrong up to the moment they start acting is the acknowledgment of a new morning, a new beginning. An example of this can be the analogy of having a favorite old and worn sweater.

Incidentally, you might continue to wear the sweater, but eventually, you realize that you want to repair it by taking the necessary action to fix it. Acknowledging is a critical piece of the puzzle; resolving and healing are essential to your journey.

It starts with your intentions – they are your compass as you navigate the healing process. Your intentions don't have to be grand or complicated, and they need to be clear and meaningful to you. It could be as simple as setting an intention each day to find peace and quiet amidst the chaos of life. Sometimes, that intention might strike in the early hours of a serene November morning when the world is still asleep or perhaps in the quiet solitude of a well-lit room on a lonely February night. Whether surrounded by familiar faces or completely alone, your intentions hold the most power in those moments.

When it comes to patience, think of hardships as storms you have to wait out. It's like steeping a tea bag and realizing the flavor needs to be stronger. Healing takes time, and self-care is often the key. Stay aware of the trap of feeling like you're back at square one or not good enough if things go differently. It's all part of the process.

Interactive Element: Journaling Prompts for Healing

Here is a series of guided journaling prompts to facilitate introspection and healing. These prompts offer space for reflection, allowing you to acknowledge your intentions, patience, and support.

1. Think back to when you felt something needed to change. What signs made you realize it was time to start healing? Were there any moments that felt like a glimmer of hope, like the first warm breeze of spring?

2. Write a letter to yourself outlining what healing means to you. Get specific about the changes you want to see in your life and how you plan to make them happen. Remember, these intentions are like seeds that will grow into your recovery journey.

3. Reflect on a time when you faced a setback in your healing journey. What challenges did you encounter, and how did you handle them? What did you learn about patience and self-compassion from this experience?

4. List the people or communities you believe can support you on your healing path. Consider reaching out to them this week, whether for a chat, a shoulder to lean on, or just some company. How can you take the first step in connecting with them?

Revisiting these prompts on a regular basis can serve as a roadmap for your healing journey. Each time you engage with them, you mark your progress and observe how the landscape of your recovery shifts and evolves.

As you navigate your recovery journey, this chapter serves not as a rigid set of rules but as a collection of guiding lights. Each guidepost is crafted to support and enlighten you along the way. Each step is a stride toward healing, from acknowledging your wounds to setting intentions, practicing patience, and seeking support. Your journey is one-of-a-kind, just like the stars in the night sky. But what connects us all is our shared resilience and the timeless quest for peace and wholeness.

The Power of Self-Reflection: Understanding Your Role

After the storm of a relationship, there's a natural pull to look inward, to sift through the layers of our thoughts and feelings. Self-reflection isn't a stroll in the park—it's more like wandering through a labyrinthine mansion, discovering new rooms and hidden passages. In these quiet moments of introspection, our soul starts a conversation with itself, exploring the tender vulnerabilities and resilient strengths within us.

Unpacking Your Emotional Baggage

In the beginning, as you begin to do your inner dialogue, you're faced with the task of unpacking your emotional baggage—a journey that requires you to be brave and honest. It's like opening an old chest filled with memories, each item holding its significance, whether it's a joyful memory or a painful one. As you sift through these artifacts, you must gently confront your vulnerabilities, acknowledging the wounds and scars they represent. But amidst this exploration, you also discover your inner strengths, often hidden beneath the weight of past struggles. Through this honest reflection on your weaknesses and strengths, you start to paint a self-portrait that reflects your genuine experiences and abilities, free from the distortions of past toxicity.

The Role of Personal Accountability

At the heart of this journey lies the practice of personal accountability, a delicate thing that has to do with owning up to your part in past relationships and avoiding the trap of self-blame. It's about understanding the importance of actions and reactions in toxic relationships. As you acknowledge moments where you may have compromised or given in, or even without drowning in feelings of guilt. Picture it like navigating a tricky mountain trail—each step forward is cautious, each recognition of a misstep balanced by an understanding of the limited choices you had at the time. Personal accountability isn't about pointing fingers; it's about seizing control of your story from the grip of past patterns.

Journaling as a Tool

In the journey of self-discovery and accountability, journaling becomes a thing you can turn to. Look at it as a safe space where you pour out your thoughts and feelings. It's not just about recording events; it's all about going more profound than that. It's about what your inner world entails and about exploring your emotions with honesty and compassion. As you put pen to paper, you give shape to your thoughts and uncover the patterns that shape your relationships and experiences. Journaling isn't just a habit—it's a form of therapy, a way to understand yourself better and find paths to healing and growth.

Growth Mindset

At the core of introspection lies the need to nurture and cultivate a growth mindset. This mindset shifts the focus from dwelling on past mistakes to seeing each experience as a chance to evolve and discover more about yourself. It infuses the process of reflection with purpose, guiding you through moments of vulnerability and strength toward greater self-awareness and resilience.

Through practices like personal accountability, journaling, and mental growth, you will reclaim who you are meant to be. It's not about returning to who you were but about forging a new path forward. Think of it as a rebirth of sorts. This journey will be challenging. It will be marked by moments of discomfort and revelation, weaving a narrative of deeply personal and universally relatable healing. It will serve as a testament to the resilience of your spirit to rise above the scars of past relationships and reach for a future filled with growth and fulfillment.

Acceptance: Facing the Reality of Your Experience

After undergoing toxic relationships, you may find yourself standing on the edge of your thoughts, facing the vast expanse of your inner world. Amidst the memories and echoes of the past, there's often a thick fog of denial, hiding the path to healing. While comforting in its familiarity, this denial also traps us, keeping us from confronting the truth of our experiences. But when you bravely confront this denial and peel back its layers with the light of awareness, you begin the journey of acceptance and transformation.

Confronting Denial

Confronting denial demands a confrontation with the self, a mirror held up to the soul to reveal the discrepancies between perceived reality and the stark truths we have, perhaps subconsciously, chosen to ignore. It is akin to navigating a labyrinth in pitch darkness, where each hesitant step forward brings us closer to the heart of our pain. This endeavor, fraught with discomfort, challenges us to acknowledge the existence of wounds we have papered over with the thin veneer of justifications and to recognize the myriad ways in which we have minimized or rationalized the toxic dynamics that once governed our lives. In this act of confrontation, we don't seek to criticize ourselves for the blindness of our past selves but to offer a hand to lead them gently into the light of understanding.

Accepting the Past

Confronting denial means facing yourself head-on, holding a mirror to your soul to uncover the gaps between what you want to believe and the harsh realities you've been avoiding. It's like navigating a maze in complete darkness, each tentative step forward bringing you closer to the heart of your pain. This process is uncomfortable, forcing you to acknowledge wounds you've tried to cover up with flimsy excuses and to admit how you've downplayed or justified the toxic patterns that once ruled your life. But in this confrontation, the goal isn't to blame yourself for past mistakes. Instead, it's about extending a compassionate hand to guide your past self into the light of understanding.

The Healing Power of Acceptance

The power of acceptance lies in its ability to free us from the grip of our past, releasing us from the burdens that have kept us stuck in resentment and regret. This freedom isn't found in dramatic moments, but in quiet realizations, in the gentle reminder from within that we're more than our past mistakes. Acceptance opens the door to a room flooded with compassion—for ourselves, the roads we've traveled, and the people we've been at every turn. With every moment of acceptance, we strengthen the essence of who we are, creating a narrative that merges the challenges of our past with the aspirations of our future.

Moving Forward

As we look ahead, we're not leaving our past behind; we're carrying it with us like a cherished old book filled with lessons and stories. It's about diving deep within ourselves, mining the gems of wisdom and strength hidden beneath the scars. Moving forward with acceptance means understanding that our past shapes who we are today.

In this journey of acceptance, we realize that our past isn't erased; it's embedded into our being. Each step taken in acceptance brings us closer to unlocking our true potential, fueled by the richness of our experiences. As you journey through recovery, you understand that acceptance is where healing and growth begin. A nurturing space fed by your experiences, fueled by your bravery to confront reality and brightened by your openness to move beyond the past.

Forgiveness: To Heal or Not to Heal

Forgiveness emerges as a profound challenge in the often turbulent journey of healing from the wounds inflicted by toxic relationships. In the realm of personal trauma and recovery, forgiveness takes on a different hue. This time, it's not just about forgiving others for the hurt they caused; it's about extending that same grace and compassion to ourselves. Self-forgiveness becomes a pivotal aspect of our healing journey. It's about acknowledging the pain you've endured, the mistakes you've made, and the lessons you've learned. By forgiving ourselves, we release the burden of self-blame and shame, allowing space for healing and growth to flourish.

Redefining Forgiveness

In this new perspective, forgiveness shifts from absolving others to freeing yourself from the emotional shackles of resentment and bitterness. It's like unclenching a fist that's held onto pain, acknowledging it without letting it define your emotional state. It's not about downplaying the seriousness of forgiveness but about reclaiming power and preserving inner peace.

Forgiveness as a Personal Choice

Forgiveness—incredibly forgiving yourself—is deeply personal and cannot be forced by external pressures. It arises from your inner dialogue, navigating feelings of guilt, regret, and eventually acceptance. It's a sacred choice that reflects your autonomy over your emotional journey.

The Role of Forgiveness in Healing

Forgiveness acts like cleansing a wound, allowing it to heal without the infection of resentment. It acknowledges past scars but diminishes their power to cause ongoing pain. Forgiveness sets you free from the cycles of anger and bitterness, restoring peace disrupted by toxic relationships.

Boundaries in Forgiveness

Forgiveness is also about setting boundaries to protect your newfound peace. It's not about holding onto grudges but about safeguarding your well-being. Forgiving while setting boundaries is a delicate balance between the heart's capacity for forgiveness and the mind's need for self-protection. It isn't an endpoint but a passage toward healing. Confronting past hurts and choosing a path toward emotional liberation requires deep self-awareness and courage. Through self-forgiveness, you navigate the complexities of toxic relationships, emerging with a heart that's open and guarded, wise and compassionate. In this space, forgiveness becomes a gift to yourself—a key to unlocking the past's chains, revealing the future's limitless potential.

The Art of Letting Go: Techniques and Practices

It becomes paramount to release the chains that bind you to memories and emotions—once sources of joy, now sources of pain—but this release demands more than a mere decision; it requires a systematic approach, a series of steps undertaken with deliberation and sensitivity.

Identifying What Holds You Back

In the quiet spaces of reflection, your first task lies in discerning those attachments that tether you to a past that no longer serves your present or promises a future. As you also hold on to material things, maybe a ring, a bracelet, a blanket, or anything physical that can bring memories, you must remember that those can sometimes hold you back. Recognizing these things for what they are—anchors tying you to the past. Sometimes, getting rid of such may be the first step toward emotional freedom. It's a meticulous process, demanding a clear eye and a willing heart. You'll have to be ready to acknowledge that not all that is held dear aids in your growth or happiness.

Mindfulness and Meditation

With the awareness of these anchors, mindfulness, and meditation provide the tools needed to maintain a presence in the now, curtailing your mind's tendency to wander back to the inevitable of "what was" and not "what currently is." In this capacity, mindfulness acts not just as a practice but as a lifeline, pulling you back from the precipice of rumination into the solid ground of the present. Through meditation, a deliberate stilling of the mind, you find the serenity necessary to focus on how you think and feel in that moment. This observation is the first step in loosening the grip of past attachments, offering clarity of mind and a tranquility of spirit that serves as the foundation for release.

Letting Go Rituals

The human psyche responds profoundly to the symbolism inherent in rituals, and it is within this framework that creating personal rituals to release the past symbolically becomes a powerful tool in the art of letting go. Unique to you, these rituals serve as a tangible act of closure, a definitive distinction between what was and will be. Whether it's the writing of letters never meant to be sent, the symbolic burning of photographs, or the gentle release of a cherished object into a flowing river, each act serves as a catharsis, a physical manifestation of an emotional release. These rituals, performed with intent and respect, honor the depth of what is being released, acknowledging its role in your life even as you choose to let it go. Some of these rituals may sound silly, but I can attest that they can be so powerful to the soul and allow your brain to process that the specific chapter in your life is over and it is time for a new beginning.

Reframing the Narrative

As we choose to let go, we mustn't take the crucial step of reshaping the story we tell ourselves about our experiences. This story, deeply ingrained in who you are, affects how you see your past, present, and what lies ahead. Reframing this narrative requires deliberately reshaping your internal dialogue and rewriting the stories you have told yourself about your worth, strength, and capacity for love and happiness. This reframing is not about denying your pain but a conscious choice to view your experiences through a lens of growth and empowerment. It's the decision to recognize that while your past relationships may have shaped you, they do not define you. Through this reframing, you permit yourself to envision a future unencumbered by the chains of past hurts. In this future, your worth is not contingent on the validation of those who could not see it, a future where you are free to forge connections that uplift rather than undermine.

As you choose to let go, these techniques and practices offer a path forward, a means by which you can gradually unburden yourself of the weights that tether you to a past that no longer serves your highest good. The journey is neither swift nor without its trials, but each step taken in mindfulness, each ritual of release, and each effort to reframe your narrative moves you closer to a place of peace and self-reclamation. In this endeavor, you find the strength to let go and the courage to move forward. You embrace the possibilities that await you, choose to release what holds you back, and open yourself to the new, the unexplored, and the yet-to-be-discovered.

Rebuilding Self-Esteem from the Ground Up

As you experience toxic relationships, you also lose your self-esteem. The fragility of your self-esteem is tested not by a single disastrous event but by the constant drip of disdain and disregard. This small, 'insignificant' overall effect slowly erodes your self-worth. The damage caused by toxic relationships isn't just surface-level—it runs deep, leaving behind scars of doubt and self-hatred. Rebuilding from this devastation starts with recognizing the extent of the damage and accepting where it comes from. The nature of relationships systematically removes the building blocks of self-esteem.

It casts uncertainty in place of the bedrock of assurance, leaving little to no doubt that one's perception of reality depends on something other than itself. Like many deceptive things, toxic relationships often hide themselves as love and concern. It's like tracing a river back to its source—you must go upstream to understand where it all begins. It goes directly against your notions of value and self to find the source.

As you choose to build yourself, we've discussed the power of affirmations. Positive self-talk is essential in rebuilding self-esteem—and nurturing the mind. Each time you say them, it's like helping you believe in them. They are meant to be meaningful and heartfelt, not just empty words. They should reflect your truth and be spoken with care. As you journey towards rebuilding, it's important to celebrate even the small victories along the way. Each moment of realization or self-acknowledgment is like adding another brick to the foundation you're building with affirmations and positive communication.

You've probably heard, "It takes 21 days to change a habit." Today, once you are done reading, you can search online and easily find videos that guide you through positive affirmations on self-love. Listen to them on the way to work on your walk, while cleaning, etc. Do this for 21 days. Begin to believe in yourself and your inner power. It's time to think you matter!

As you count your victories, they are small but demonstrate the successful establishment of a boundary or a day lived without hiding from yourself. Celebrating these small victories generates and maintains an eternal belief in one's capacity to let go and change, becoming increasingly self-aware.

As you go through this change, it may seem a little funky. You might question yourself: am I searching for outside validation? Not at all! You are looking for internal validation, one that learns to accept yourself for who you are by re-programming your mind. Such re-programming occurs within toxic relationships and their power structures, as they drag people into depending on the opinion of others about themselves.

Toxic relationships are just so detrimental to one's health. They diminish your whole sense of self-worth. It is often seen that victims of toxic environments must dedicate themselves to their internal emotional processes, building routines and thought patterns with the steady intent to believe in themselves. People claim that the inner voice echoes the outside presentations, however loud it is. Yet, in reality, the inner voice is the one that fades away faster than others, not to become a permanent addition to one's system.

As you rebuild yourself, you will distinguish numerous related and dependent stages, timewise and resultant. Self-esteem progress and development as a symbol of building and striving to a new order is a multistage process where every step counts. You'll eventually realize that the process is highly time-absorbing, requiring significant effort and time. Despite this, every step forward and any slight dedication and self-assurance achievement can be seen as another way out of the toxic legacy of the past. As you let go, you gradually transform into a new reality where your self-esteem is highly improved.

Cultivating Resilience: Lessons in Strength

Rebounding from toxic relationships takes a lot of inner strength. It's more like using the energy from all your bad experiences into something that makes you stronger. But you do have to remember that it's never about returning to how things used to be. It's more like a landscape reshaped by storms - still powerful, but different. Building resilience means finding emotional strength, learning from what you've been through, and creating a whole new you.

To build emotional resilience, you must also work on your emotional intelligence. It refers to working through feelings and navigating emotions gracefully and informally. For example, mindfulness is a powerful technique to carry in the storm of regressive thinking—at any given time, the mind could cling back to the "normal" stance you had. It remains fresh in the past. Emotional regulation matters more than you can imagine, requiring a lot of focus and work.

It is also crucial for you to not just go through experiences but learn from them. It's easy to sometimes go with the flow, but someone who will take something out of what they went through has to also analyze and rethink with an open mind. It sounds easier said than done, as it requires your willingness to change and move on. The process of relevance powerfully relies on the retrospection of the past. No matter how fracturing and painful each relationship was, it gives those involved something of learning value. There is always a note for future decisions and attributes to the relationship with others. After multiple failed relationships, you can look back and see what they should avoid or do in the future. Emotional resilience is like a compass guiding your growth and transformation into the person you aspire to be. It's forged in the fires of adversity, laying a sturdy foundation for rebuilding yourself into a stronger, more whole individual.

Self-Care: More Than Just a Buzzword

The damage that toxic relationships cause leaves a trail of issues that continue to linger. For this reason, it is vital to address the concept of 'self-care' as it emerges again, not as a passing trend but as an essential component of personal healing. It goes beyond mere indulgence, recognizing self-care as a crucial and diverse practice for emotional recovery. From simple practices like mindful breathing to more complex strategies like setting boundaries, each technique plays a role in the tapestry of your healing process.

A common trait of each self-care technique is the imperative of gentle attention to a person's bodily and mental needs. This gentle attention translates into thin and acute awareness of the subtle signals of the body and mind. It follows up by permitting those signals the time and attention they need. The technique can be extended to the art of preparing a garden for the growth of selected plants, with some preferring the warmth of the sun and others the coolness of shade. Similarly, self-care is best conducted by gentle attentiveness to encourage an environment in which you can flourish. Know that even five minutes to yourself counts! Start slow and give yourself the time you deserve.

Routines have such a critical role in self-care practice that their potential to provide the conditions under which the building of well-being can occur is so significant. Routines fix regular behavior patterns, but these behaviors should be conceptualized as something other than the confinement of unrestrained freedom into a schedule. Instead, they provide a predictable rhythm amid recovery's propensity for chaos and wildness, echoing the steady rhythms of the heart within the tumult of existence. These practices encompass rituals such as morning meditation, grounding individuals in inner peace and reflection to navigate the challenges of the day ahead.

When a toxic relationship is over, it is like a hurricane swept through both parties, leaving destruction behind. At such times, taking care of yourself is a powerful act of independence and a protest against the overall notion. Developing a long-term relationship with yourself after undergoing so much trauma over again should be a must. When you get caught up in the pain of a toxic relationship, taking care of yourself appears to be a type of intimate evaluation. Few dare to speak their feelings without shame.

Nevertheless, it often seems like dropping to the floor and not getting up. This type of rebellion is more like a muted whisper with the impact of a scream. Soil resists the roots of plants attempting to emerge from the ground, convincing them not to grow. Simultaneously, a revelation of a personalized plan to handle self-care challenges becomes a silent shout about your worth and right to be happy.

A personalized self-care program serves as a survival strategy, mapping out the journey through the peaks and valleys of trauma. While attention may be fixed on the "hills" of past experiences, it's essential to be prepared for the unseen "declines." For some, reconnecting with physical activities like exercise, sports, dancing, or experimenting with new foods can awaken the senses and provide comfort. Meanwhile, others may find solace in moments of solitude, where they can be themselves and unwind with genuine "Me time."

As you establish your plan, consider your preferences; what guides you to your deepest level? The recognition of such preferences, from the type of activities to the choice of boundaries, must be aimed at reiterating the importance of your autonomy in the healing process. This healing implies honesty and courage, the ability to recognize your boundaries, and the readiness to state your needs in an environment where you are constantly expected to be productive and self-sacrificing. This customized way of self-care is more than a tool for ensuring your well-being; it is a profound way of self-discovery and self-affirmation.

Self-care is an integral part of your life; it reminds many of the power and independence that returning to your true self can do. It is the part of the narrative that leads to human recovery. It is not limited to the cessation of tortures but is about establishing an abundant, meaningful, and appropriate life. In learning to care for yourself, you're not just healing the wounds of the past but laying the groundwork for a future where your happiness and peace are top priorities. From this perspective, self-care moves beyond being just another trendy term and becomes a sacred practice, symbolizing both the necessity and the privilege of your healing journey. Recognizing the profound significance of self-care leads us to explore why we must also use the support systems available.

Finding Your Tribe: The Importance of Support Systems

After everything that happened, when our heads are full of dozens of conflicting thoughts, and when our hearts are heavy with issues, we no longer feel a strong connection to anyone or anything. We often seek solitude as a coping mechanism. However, as the dust settles and we start to process what happened, we long for comfort and for our feelings to resonate with someone. It is at this point that communities become relevant. These virtual and physical areas are created and populated by people who know what you are going through and offer their understanding and empathy.

When you seek out a support group or some other community that can provide you with the support you desperately need, it can feel like walking through a dense forest. There is no clear path, just slight hints pointing you in the right direction. Once you leave the forest behind, you can see a beautiful, comprehensive clearing before you. Here, support groups, whether online or neighborhood meetups, offer new ways of thinking. By talking to people who have been in the same position you are in, you learn not just about your experiences but about the multitudes of ways people deal with their issues. What follows is a collection of stories from many such people who have fought battles but whose strategies apply to just as many people.

In our digital age, it's easy to equate the number of connections we have with the depth of our relationships. We're bombarded with daily interactions, but proper support isn't found in the quantity of acquaintances but in the quality of a few meaningful connections. These genuine relationships offer a kind of nourishment that's hard to come by. They're the conversations that last for hours, the shared moments of laughter, and the silent understanding between two people. While setting boundaries with family members can be challenging, it's essential for maintaining healthy relationships. It's not always easy, but it's crucial for our well-being.

Through the biological connections that bind us, our chosen family is one of the brightest lights. Family is selected instead of given, bound by mutual respect, understanding, and love. They highlight the best parts of what families can be but frequently need more. Instead of adhering to a given set of predetermined roles, family is often one of acceptance and celebration—a place where you can be your true self. Family is perhaps more impactful than any other bond or tool for deep emotion because it is created. These bonds are rooted in a shared commitment to each other's personal growth, happiness, and mutual support. Support communities, deep bonds, family dynamics, and chosen family connections collectively provide a strong foundation of support for the recovery journey. In these supports, we see not just ourselves but the possibility of future narratives of our strength and warmth, support and health, and the loving bonds we form to grow.

Professional Help: When to Seek Therapy

When you're navigating the twists and turns of healing from toxic relationships, having a guide—a seasoned companion—to help you through the complexities of the journey can make all the difference. Therapy serves as that guiding light, illuminating the path to healing with the expertise of science and the compassion of art. Choosing to seek professional help is a significant step, marked by subtle realizations; it's an acknowledgment that your emotional burdens have become too heavy to bear alone and now require the expertise and support of a professional.

Recognizing the Need for Professional Support

Have you felt stuck, where days blur together without any sense of progress or overwhelming emotions overshadowing any joy or connection you used to feel? Such are signs that it's time to consider therapy. In these moments, when the internal chaos drowns out the rhythm of daily life, your soul calls out for help. Recognizing these signs requires a pause, a moment of stillness to listen closely to your inner voice and acknowledge the need for support beyond what you can provide yourself.

Therapy as a Tool for Healing

In therapy, the bond between you and your therapist creates a unique space where various strategies are customized to fit your unique story, emotions, and goals for recovery. Whether it's cognitive-behavioral techniques to shift negative thinking patterns or delving into past experiences with psychodynamic approaches, therapy flexes to meet your needs. This tailored approach ensures that your journey toward healing isn't a generic path, but a personalized route designed with your history, personality, and dreams in mind.

Overcoming Stigma

The choice to pursue therapy is often clouded by the shadow of societal stigma—a lingering fear that seeking mental health support signifies weakness or failure. I am sure you've heard that those who do therapy must have mental issues. In reality, we all have something, big or small, to work through. We all need the help of a professional to guide us. This outdated stigma creates obstacles to healing, portraying therapy as a sign of fragility rather than bravery. Overcoming this stigma requires a change in conversation, both within yourself and among those around you. It is vital to acknowledge therapy as a valuable investment in your well-being. It's an act of self-care that demonstrates strength, resilience, and a dedication to personal growth. Choosing therapy is reclaiming your power and affirming that your mental health deserves professional care and attention above all else.

Finding the Right Therapist

Looking for the right therapist is like setting out on an adventure into unknown territory—it takes time and careful consideration. You're not just looking for someone with the right qualifications; you're searching for someone you'll connect with, someone you can trust and open up to. A few tips for finding the right fit involve seeking therapists who specialize in the areas you need help with. Ask friends or family for recommendations, and don't hesitate to schedule a few initial consultations to see if you feel comfortable with them. And always trust your gut—if something feels off, keep looking until you find the therapist who feels like the perfect match, someone who makes you feel safe and supported.

As we reflect on this chapter's journey, we see therapy not just as an extra tool in the healing toolbox but as a cornerstone—a vital foundation for rebuilding yourself. While healing is deeply personal, it should not be a solo mission. Seeking professional help means having a knowledgeable, empathetic companion by your side, someone dedicated to helping you navigate the highs and lows that come from the recovery process. As we wrap up our exploration of therapy's role, we understand that healing is like a mosaic. Each piece—whether it's self-care, support from loved ones, or guidance from a therapist—is essential to the bigger picture.

CHAPTER 4

Setting Boundaries: A Path to Self-Preservation and Respect

B oundaries are personal limits we set to protect our overall well-being, physical and emotional. They define what is acceptable and what isn't in our interactions with others. Through boundaries, we make sure that our needs and feelings are guarded. It's about saying "no" when we need to and being transparent about what makes us comfortable or uncomfortable.

The Basics of Boundaries

Boundaries are essential to protecting yourself from anyone who may come along with malice and hurt you. They are the voice you use when you are standing for yourself. Believe me when I say this: Anyone can be run over without boundaries. Being firm in what you stand for and your beliefs is essential. By setting boundaries, you are protecting the sanctity of your inner world, fostering healthy connections while keeping toxicity away.

Types of Boundaries

You set boundaries to define what is acceptable and unacceptable in how others interact with you. Boundaries come in various forms, addressing different aspects of your life. Emotional boundaries safeguard your feelings and thoughts, while physical boundaries protect your personal space and bodily autonomy. Today, we can only talk about boundaries with our involvement with technology and social media. Why do I say this? I mention this because the digital world is like open doors and, if unshielded, may affect our overall well-being. In various cases, those in control within toxic relationships may use the digital world as a form of control. Who you talk to, what you post, and how you post essentially rob you of your voice and persona. Setting boundaries involves standing up for yourself, your privacy, and the right to manage your digital realm.

Rights Within Relationships

Every relationship has an unspoken contract of mutual respect and understanding. You have the inherent right to express your needs, voice discomfort, and expect respect. It's like being the author of a book; you decide the narrative and who plays a role in your life.

Boundaries as Self-Respect

Setting boundaries is an act of self-respect and self-preservation. It affirms that your peace, safety, and dignity matter. Setting boundaries is important because you also set yourself up as high as you set boundaries! You are worth it, and you can demand respect. Unfortunately, in toxic relationships, boundaries are the decisions that can keep you from losing yourself. Boundaries are the way to nurture your growth and protect your essence.

The importance of self-preservation and boundary setting became evident through research on the growing trend of working from home since the COVID-19 Pandemic. The study examined blurred work-life boundaries' impact on lifestyle and subjective well-being. The findings led to two very important factors that affected happiness. One found that healthy overall lifestyle patterns buffered employees against the detrimental effects of blurred work-life boundaries and emotional exhaustion on happiness (Plutt, Wonders, 2020). The other factor showed that employees who experienced increases in the blurring of work-life boundaries reported a deterioration in healthy lifestyle behaviors, which in turn was related to reduced happiness (Plutt, Wonders, 2020).

As you can see from this study, the lack of a boundary setting can impact your emotional health. The truth is, there are more studies out there that prove that the lack of a boundary setting can be harmful to your well-being. Establishing boundaries may take time because of how we were raised. Some of our parents must not have taught us what it means to put them into practice. Letting others treat us a certain way can be a habit, and we often do it without realizing we are digging ourselves into a hole. Practice them, learn them, and make them a part of you.

Visual Element: Infographic on Types of Boundaries

Consider declining an invitation to an event that brings more stress than joy. It's not a dismissal of friendship but a prioritization of your well-being. This act is a testament to understanding that as you say "no" to others, you say "yes" to yourself. In these small yet significant moments, you master the art of boundary-setting, enriching your interactions and enhancing your existence.

The Process of Setting Boundaries

Understanding your boundaries becomes crucial. It's not just about self-inquiry; it's about delving deep into your soul's calling. Such involves uncovering values, experiences, and comfort levels buried under societal expectations and personal history. Each of us has a unique blend of past encounters and intrinsic values. We all hold a distinct set of thresholds that mark where comfort ends and discomfort begins. Identifying these boundaries demands acute awareness of your emotional and physical responses and a willingness to confront and accept these truths without judgment.

Communicating Your Boundaries

Once you've unearthed your boundaries, the next step is to share them with the world. It's not a simple task; it's a deliberate act of self-assertion that requires clarity and conviction. Expressing your boundaries demands clear language, leaving no room for misinterpretation. Knowing your limits is not enough, but it would help if you articulated them assertively yet respectfully. This conversation, though vulnerable, becomes less daunting when approached with the understanding that it's not a demand but a declaration of self-respect.

Enforcing Your Boundaries

Declaring boundaries is just the beginning. The real challenge lies in enforcing them against external resistance and internal doubt. Enforcing a boundary means safeguarding your well-being against disrespect and violation. It involves active engagement and, sometimes, confrontation. At this phase, you must defend your boundaries consistently. Sporadically defending a boundary undermines its credibility.

Adjusting Your Boundaries as Needed

Boundaries aren't rigid constructs but living entities that evolve with you. Recognizing that boundaries may shift in response to new experiences and insights is crucial. This adaptability signifies growth and the ability to reassess and recalibrate boundaries as needed. Adjusting a boundary is an exercise in self-reflection and forgiveness, acknowledging that needs and tolerances change over time. Though challenging, this process underscores the dynamic nature of personal development and the ongoing dialogue between yourself and the world.

As you learn to understand the nature of relationships, setting, communicating, enforcing, and adjusting boundaries will guide you through self-discovery and empowerment. Boundary setting demands awareness, assertiveness, compassion, and grace as you honor your boundaries and those of others.

Communicating Your Boundaries Effectively

Assertive communication is not about overpowering your partner or stepping back timidly; it's finding that perfect balance where you express yourself firmly yet respectfully. Assertive communication means speaking up for yourself without feeling guilty or aggressive, making sure your voice is heard and respected in the conversation. Being assertive helps you draw the line, letting others know where you stand without ambiguity.

Avoiding Apologies for Boundaries

Sometimes, setting boundaries can feel like apologizing for taking up space or asking for what you need. But remember, asserting your boundaries is not something you should feel sorry for. It's about recognizing your worth and standing up for yourself without guilt. Setting boundaries is a way of honoring your own needs and values. No, you shouldn't have to apologize for that. Instead, embrace the fact that you prioritize your well-being and show respect for yourself and your relationships.

Handling Pushback

When you set boundaries, it's natural to face some resistance or pushback from others. But dealing with this doesn't have to be confrontational or stressful. Stay firm in your boundaries while keeping the lines of communication open. Explain your reasons calmly and listen to the other person's perspective with empathy. Finding common ground and compromise is critical, but never compromise your well-being or values. Stay true to yourself and stand your ground when necessary.

The Role of Non-Verbal Communication

Communication isn't just about your words; it's also about how you say them and the messages your body language sends. Non-verbal cues like eye contact, posture, and facial expressions convey confidence and assertiveness (Robinson, 2023). Please pay attention to your body language and make sure it aligns with the message you're trying to convey. A strong and confident stance can reinforce your boundaries and show others you mean business.

Dealing with Boundary Violations

In the overall context of relationships between people, boundary violations often look like a subtle pattern of disrespect. In many cases, such violations appear in the form of seemingly rational affection or careful treatment. Boundary violations, however, encroach upon the territory of our personal space, escalating our need for both an immediate response and some degree of self-contemplation. The ability to identify such violations requires strong self-awareness and a recognition of our motivations and intentions. Acknowledging such is the first step in reclaiming your wrongly appropriated property. Boundary violations are essential to your experience and the skills necessary for maintaining a healthy sense of yourself.

Boundary violations can be unnoticeable and leave you with discomfort and emotional uneasiness. In many cases, the signals are overlooked, misjudged, or disregarded. When someone disregards your needs or acts carelessly, it's common to try to justify their behavior with pseudo-rational explanations. But recognizing when your boundaries have been crossed takes a finely tuned intuition and the bravery to trust your feelings. Speaking up about these violations is crucial; it helps draw clear lines around your boundaries, reducing the chances of others stepping over them repeatedly.

Immediate Responses

When someone crosses your boundaries, your initial reaction is often a surge of tension, calling for an assertive and respectful response. You might address the violation right then and there, verbally or through your body language, as a clear indication of what's unacceptable. Such could be a simple but firm statement like, "I'm not comfortable with that," or "Please respect my boundaries." While it might feel uncomfortable to confront the situation, it's important to remember that this isn't about being aggressive; it's about asserting your rights. You have every right to stand up for yourself and express your limits. And there's no need to apologize afterward; you were defending your boundaries. This initial reaction addresses the immediate issue and sets a precedent for future interactions, letting others know you won't tolerate boundary violations.

Long-term Strategies

When boundary violations become recurring, especially from the same individuals, it's time to take a more strategic, long-term approach. It might mean reassessing the relationship and weighing the benefits of staying connected against the costs of ongoing disrespect. It could involve having honest, open conversations about boundaries in a safe environment where both parties can share their perspectives and find common ground. Sometimes, it may even require physical or emotional distance to protect your well-being. While distancing yourself from someone you care about can be difficult, it's a reminder that your self-respect should always come first. In other words, when you prioritize your well-being over seeking approval from others, you acknowledge your value. If someone repeatedly violates your boundaries, it's a clear sign of disrespect, and such behavior is unlikely to change without significant intervention. In these moments, the focus shifts from salvaging the relationship to prioritizing your self-preservation. It's a tough decision, but a deep respect for your worth and dignity drives it.

Self-care after a violation

After your boundaries have been violated, taking care of yourself feels essential – a way to ease the sting of feeling disregarded. Yet, this self-care isn't just about treating yourself; it's a vital part of healing – a return to your core after experiencing disrespect. It could involve doing things that bring you joy and comfort, like engaging in activities that nurture your soul or taking a quiet day to reflect and process your feelings. This self-care reminds you of your inner power and the strength to rebuild yourself after others have crossed your boundaries. It's not about being demanding; it's about gathering yourself together – an act of self-repair for the emotional wounds inflicted.

This self-care also acts as a form of preparation, making future boundary violations less painful by fortifying your emotional resilience. Managing boundary violations involves making choices that may not seem monumental at the time. Each step in the process requires clear, deliberate decisions. Self-awareness must be paired with firmness to enforce your boundaries. These actions are courageous not because they're inherently difficult but because they're simultaneously significant and subtle, directed inward rather than outward. By managing your boundaries, you're shielding yourself and actively affirming your inherent worth and value.

Boundaries in Digital Relationships

Establishing boundaries is crucial yet frequently neglected in our expansive digital world. With its vastness and captivating allure, the online realm poses challenges and opportunities to define personal space and privacy. Amid the constant stream of information and connectivity, navigating online interactions requires individuals to create havens of solitude and respect amidst the digital commotion.

Digital Boundaries: The Cartography of Online Space

Digital boundaries, much like those in our offline relationships, delineate our virtual territories, marking the boundaries of our openness and the extent of our exposure. However, these boundaries require a unique mapping process, considering the fluidity and permeability of online interactions. Setting digital boundaries involves deliberate demarcation, deciding what aspects of our lives we share and which we keep private. It's a defense against the erosion of privacy in the face of digital voyeurism and exhibitionism. This process entails a constant negotiation between the desire for connection and the need for confidentiality, striving to maintain the integrity of our digital identities.

Social Media and Privacy: Navigating the Public Square

Social media platforms serve as today's public squares, posing a unique challenge for maintaining digital boundaries. Here, where private and public realms converge, managing privacy settings becomes paramount in safeguarding personal boundaries. Customizing these settings to suit your comfort level transforms social media platforms from open books to putting up the wall, where you have complete control over the extent and nature of interactions (Flintoff, 2023). This reflective sharing isn't about deceit; it's about asserting independence, declaring that you alone decide which parts of your life are showcased to the world and which remain secluded in the realm of privacy.

Online Communication: The Etiquette of Digital Discourse

Online communication takes an almost infinite number of forms beyond social media, from texting to messaging apps and beyond. The immediacy of such communication, coupled with its essentially overdue nature, relies on adding a willing recipient. It renders it in a unique gray area where the total bandwidth of interpersonal communication etiquette does not quite hold. Etiquette of digital discourse is a new, essential set of rules that delineate the temporal dimension of ultimate acceptability regarding time recruitment for responses and exert a cautionary note on the appropriateness of unsolicited communication. It asserts the right to disengage whenever you deem fit. It is an admission that behind the screen is an actual person who deserves to be respected as such.

Cyber harassment is a conflict that can erupt in the online world. It occurs due to bullying, stalking, and threatening other people on the Internet. Some people take advantage of the digital world to feel impunity and superiority. The likely victims are those who share their pictures and videos on social networks, websites, or dating apps. It can severely affect their self-esteem and often lead to suicide. It can be such an intense topic, as it becomes very mental for many. If your boundaries online have been broken, it is so important to seek out professional help. Depending on the scenario, such cases may often go to court along with sufficient evidence. Nevertheless, it is essential to try to control anger and stress because, in many cases, cyber harassment could be an unconscious behavior.

When facing such a distressing situation, you might resort to various tactics to protect yourself. Blocking all communication with the individual involved could be a necessary step to safeguard your well-being. Additionally, gathering evidence and reporting the cyber-harassment to the social network's administration and law enforcement authorities is crucial to address the issue effectively. Pursuing legal action through the court may also be necessary to seek justice and ensure the safety of those affected while holding the perpetrators accountable for their actions. In such situations, accommodation or negotiation tactics may not be feasible, especially when dealing with individuals who continue to harm others without regard for their well-being.

The Role of Boundaries in Self-Respect

As we empower the boundaries we set, we shout their importance and how much we truly value, respect, and cherish ourselves. Setting these boundaries isn't just about managing interactions; it's an intimate dialogue with ourselves, where we explore the essence of our self-regard and the vastness of our self-esteem. At this point, you should know that it's crucial to step back and say no—not as a complete denial, but as an affirmation of our right to have needs and boundaries. It's the moment to pause and assert to the universe that "my well-being is not negotiable; my comfort is not a commodity to be sacrificed for the peace of others."

From the sturdy foundation of self-respect, our quest for empowerment flourishes in the fertile ground of boundary setting and enforcement. This empowerment isn't a rigid fortress shielding us from the world; it's more like a guiding lighthouse, illuminating our path as we navigate interpersonal relationships. It leads us towards interactions based not on submission or dominance but mutual respect and understanding.

That's why boundary setting can be so empowering, especially regarding enforcement. Through boundaries, we don't try to be someone else or act in ways that contradict our true selves. Instead, we become integrated beings whose thoughts, emotions, and intentions align with our words and actions. Boundaries allow us to safeguard our needs and limitations, and those who disregard them are left behind. It's a journey of empowerment where we refuse to let our past, moods, or others dictate our course; instead, we live in a present that we create for ourselves.

There are often old beliefs that creep back into our everyday life. Sometimes, Old habits don't go away and stay deep in our minds. Those thoughts harm our worthiness and warn us of the dangers of asserting ourselves. These beliefs tell us that looking inward and understanding ourselves is off-limits. It's so important not to conform to the expectations of others but to maintain the image they've created for us to be accepted and loved. But what if these beliefs are outdated and no longer serve us? What if those who disrespect our boundaries don't truly belong in our lives? In that case, these ideas are false notions holding us back. The only way to truly flourish is to dig deep into our being and uproot these harmful beliefs, one by one, no matter how much effort it takes to nurture our growth.

Don't think of boundaries as barriers but as bridges, connections that can make our relationships with others at once honest, reasonable, and rewarding. They invite others to meet us, not halfway, but in a place where we can regard each other equally. Boundaries bring us to a space where the exchange between them and us is not a compromise but a cooperation, not a sacrifice but shared joy. To dare and challenge old beliefs is to free ourselves from the bonds of conditioning and offer others the chance to engage with us more genuinely and less demandingly. As you go through this journey, you'll send a powerful message to those in your lives. We inhabit spaces of authenticity and respect where everyone's needs and boundaries are honored.

Boundaries and self-respect don't isolate us; they shape a world of relationships that reflect how much we truly accept ourselves. As we establish and refine these boundaries, we witness our self-esteem mirrored in the quality of the relationships we choose to nurture. It isn't selfishness; it's care. By confining ourselves to sound and wholesome spaces, we allow others to do the same. The true role of boundaries in self-respect: doubly sturdy as both protection and invitation. They shield us from madness and guide the world and its people toward a place of equal regard and mutual benefit.

Navigating Boundaries with Family and Friends

Families and friends hold some of the dearest spots in our hearts, underscoring their significance in countless aspects of our lives. Whether we need them or they need us, their presence is invaluable and deeply cherished. However, within such closest circles, the issue of setting boundaries may become most acute. Regarding family dynamics, the challenges sometimes need to be clarified. They're often tangled up in years of shared experiences and emotions. For many, just figuring out the problem can feel like an uphill battle, let alone finding a solution that works. It takes more than just knowledge of family dynamics to tackle these issues effectively. It would help if you also had a keen sense of the shifting boundaries and emotions involved, like navigating through choppy waters.

Families

Family relationships can be so complex, right? It's like this big, tangled mess of personalities, histories, and shared moments. Sometimes, it feels like we're all just blending into one another, making it hard to figure out where one story ends and another begins. It takes a lot of care and attention to navigate all that is like trying to trim a garden without cutting the flowers. We're constantly balancing being close and having our own space, staying loyal while still being true to ourselves. Understanding where we fit into this family puzzle is vital, ensuring we nurture each connection while respecting everyone's boundaries. It's not about being selfish; it's about having honest conversations and making sure everyone feels heard and respected so we can grow together healthily.

You know, family dynamics can get messy as we grow older. We're all trying to find our place in this ever-changing puzzle, but sometimes, the pieces just don't fit quite right. Maybe you're feeling overwhelmed by everyone depending on you, or perhaps there's that one sibling who always seems to stir up trouble, leaving a trail of hurt feelings and unresolved issues. It's tough when family relationships start to feel toxic. Setting boundaries with family members can be easier said than done.

But here's the thing: putting your well-being first isn't selfish—it's necessary. Sometimes, creating space between yourself and your family can be the healthiest choice. It's about prioritizing your mental and emotional health and ultimately paving the way for a brighter, more fulfilling future.

Carl's Family Story

Carl grew up in a household where tension was a constant undercurrent. His parents' volatile relationship set the tone for daily life, filled with arguments, accusations, and emotional manipulation. His father, in particular, belittled Carl, using harsh words to diminish his self-worth. His mother, caught in her own struggles, was often distant, leaving Carl alone to navigate the emotional minefield. To this date, he believes his mom would probably have been better if she received the needed help.

Carl felt he needed to be the peacemaker growing up to keep the household from erupting into chaos. But this role came at a cost. He felt like he constantly walked on eggshells, his self-esteem eroding yearly. The toxic environment seeped into his psyche, making him believe that he was undeserving of love and respect.

As Carl grew older, he started to see the patterns of dysfunction more clearly. The realization hit him hard when he found himself replicating similar toxic dynamics in his relationships. He recognized that he had absorbed the negativity from his parents and was unconsciously playing out those same roles. It was a painful awakening but also a necessary one.

Determined to break free from the cycle, Carl made a brave decision to distance himself from his family early in his 30s. It wasn't easy. The guilt and fear of abandoning his parents weighed heavily on him, as he knew they were getting older. But Carl knew that for his own mental health and future happiness, he needed to create space.

Carl moved to a different city, seeking a fresh start. He began therapy, where he unpacked the layers of his past, understanding how deeply the toxicity had affected him. Through therapy, Carl learned about healthy boundaries and the importance of self-care. He started to rebuild his self-esteem slowly but surely.

In his new environment, Carl prioritized surrounding himself with positive influences. He joined support groups and made friends who valued and respected him—sought out mentors who guided him toward personal growth. With time, he started to build healthier relationships based on mutual respect and understanding.

He realized that distancing himself from his toxic family didn't mean he didn't care about them; he cared enough about himself to prioritize his well-being. As Carl sat across from me and told me his story, his eyes got watery, and I could feel the pain he had endured and how he had tried so hard to transform his life. Carl reclaimed his life by choosing to distance himself and paved the way for a future filled with healthier, more fulfilling relationships.

Carl's story may connect with you, and you may have endured a similar situation. As not everyone can move away, know that boundaries are crucial to who you allow to enter your mental state.

Friendships

Navigating friendships is like exploring a vast landscape of twists and turns, challenges, and hidden treasures. Friendships are unique because we choose them. Unlike family relationships, where boundaries can sometimes feel predetermined, friendships give us the freedom to define our limits. It's a chance to practice assertiveness and communicate our needs openly without the weight of expectation. But even in these chosen relationships, clear communication is critical. Being honest about our boundaries creates a foundation built on trust and respect. It's about nurturing a space where both parties feel heard, valued, and understood, fostering a bond that can weather any storm.

Toxic friendships? Unfortunately, they're all too familiar. We've all had that friend who seemed to bring more drama than joy. Let's dive into two scenarios that might sound familiar. Think back to middle or high school. Remember that friend or group who didn't respect your boundaries? Maybe they were the popular crowd, and you felt like you had to stick with them to fit in. They make you feel guilty for spending time with others, brushing off your feelings, and never taking responsibility for their actions. Sound familiar?

Now, let's jump ahead. You've moved on from those toxic friendships and found new ones. But maybe you still have friends who drain your energy, constantly need something from you, or say hurtful things. You replicate negative interactions in your head even when you're not with them. These friends might bring toxic vibes into your life without you even realizing it. Recognizing the signs of toxicity is the first step. It's crucial to stand up for yourself and voice your feelings and needs. Setting boundaries in every relationship is key to maintaining mental and emotional well-being. It's not about shutting people out; it's about creating healthy, respectful connections where both parties feel valued and heard.

Cultural Considerations

Culture adds another layer of complexity within family and friendship, shaping how we view and approach boundaries. From the stories we hear as children to the customs we practice as adults, culture influences our ideas of what's acceptable and respected in our relationships and what is not. Navigating boundaries in this mix requires us to be mindful of these cultural influences and recognize their impact on our actions and expectations. Navigating the intersection of tradition and personal boundaries can feel like walking on a tightrope. While some of us hold our cultural traditions close to our hearts, others might have a more cynical view of relationships due to their experiences.

In today's world, it's becoming increasingly common to hear stories of divorce or broken families. I am sure that a lot of us have seen our parents or someone we love go through failed relationships, which can leave a lasting impression. We've been taught that relationships are fleeting and that finding lasting love is a fairy tale. Others might never experience that, but they become scared to give in as they meet others because they fear the what-ifs.

Here's the thing: We bring our unique blend of flavors, backgrounds, and experiences to the table. Our life experiences shape the culture within our families and our relationships with our partners, kids, and friends. It's essential to recognize how our past influences how we navigate boundaries and relationships and to be mindful of how we can create a healthy balance between what we are used to, our traditions, and personal autonomy.

Setting boundaries with loved ones might be difficult, but know it matters! And it truly matters because you are standing up for yourself. It can get complicated when resistance gets in the way, and it comes from your own family or friends. It's not just an obstacle; it's like looking in a mirror that reflects your fears, doubts, and the strength of your boundaries. To push back against this resistance, you must approach it delicately, with compassion and assertiveness. Understand that the issue might not be the boundaries themselves but what they represent – shifts in dynamics, renegotiation of roles, and changes in how you relate to each other.

Through active listening, you hear what someone is saying and are attuned to their thoughts and feelings (Gallo, 2024). It turns a conversation into an active, non-competitive, two-way interaction. It's a reminder that relationships aren't static; they're living entities that can change and grow.

As you become more aware of the toxicity some people bring into your life, it's natural to feel a mix of emotions for them—perhaps care, concern, or even love. But it's crucial to recognize that clear boundaries define healthy relationships. As you nurture your relationships and offer support, remember to uphold your limits consistently. It isn't just about respecting yourself; it's also about showing care for others. In my view, this is the foundation for fostering and cherishing meaningful connections.

Setting Boundaries in The Workplace

The theme of boundaries in the workplace is vitally important for many and is even more relevant in the professional context. Although sometimes friends, colleagues, or managers don't pay enough attention to an individual's private space, boundaries should still be defined. Professional boundaries should serve as a foundation to remind everyone where to stop. They are the invisible, yet strong, traits between collaboration and complete submersion into a professional that is not desirable. Therefore, these notions should be perfectly balanced for personal and coworker relationships.

Professional responsibilities and personal boundaries from the workplace represent the establishment of self-boundaries as much as they are reflections of your professional attitude. It is an acknowledgment that careers require time, place, and attention, but they don't necessarily claim our lives. It does not diminish the dedication to your work; rather, it facilitates the fulfillment of our roles from a place of ease and happiness. The inflow of energy and effort remains intact. Harmony ensures that the outflow of labor is equally vibrant and sustainable, with personal well-being as the backbone of your professional contributions.

Navigating the balance between work and personal life can be challenging, but it comes with challenges. The lines between work and personal life are becoming increasingly blurred due to an increase in remote and hybrid work. Setting clear boundaries for your work hours, communication channels, and physical and digital productive spaces helps build a supportive environment and sets the stage for the performance that is our professional lives. The boundaries set in your professional setting eventually trickle down to your personal life.

Creating and maintaining these boundaries can be challenging, especially when colleagues or supervisors cross them without realizing it. Whether through unreasonable expectations of availability outside office hours or inquiries into one's personal life, these transgressions must be addressed, and doing so requires a delicate blend of assertiveness and diplomacy. It is a communication approach that makes one's boundaries clear while maintaining the professional respect and decorum that a workplace requires. In this sense, it is a negotiation conducted as a diplomatic mission, where engagement terms are redefined to give our boundaries the honor they deserve to protect our well-being.

When negotiating these boundaries, it's crucial to advocate for yourself. Indeed, the acquisition and practice of workplace boundaries are a self-advocacy skill. It is not a matter of simply asking what you want. Instead, self-advocacy is better understood as an exercise in educating others about our values on our time, mental space, and energy. It takes a more nuanced understanding of workplace dynamics and culture than expected and a higher level of confidence and assertiveness. We must clarify that our needs must be met to help others, but we do it not out of personal whim but because we are more effective professionals when they are met. It creates a workplace culture in which the next person demands to be treated equally. Respect, balance, and regard for well-being – and one's workplace contributes not by forcing or guilt-tripping but by supporting those boundaries.

As we deal with professional interactions, we can easily see the ambition, duty, and magnitude of people who often try to get to the top of the pyramid. Due to their complexity, setting your boundaries and seeing them as walls that protect you from others is important. They denote the areas where the professional personal ends and personal identity begins, guaranteeing that our vocation enriches rather than diminishes us. Through the establishment of professional boundaries, the maintenance of work-life equilibrium, the negotiation of overextending colleagues, and the exercise of self-advocacy, we develop not merely our career triumphs but our well-being.

Let's face it, workplaces are like their own little world. We are always on the go, egotistic personalities emerge, and cliques are formed. In other words, it can often feel like a place of competition for many. Because work environments set their own culture, you must recognize at least the culture and how human relations unfold. The example below shows Jessica's struggle as she deals with a toxic environment and a toxic boss.

Jessica's Story

I have a friend who stands up for herself and others. She's one to take a stance and will rise for what she believes in. Jessica, who had just landed a job at a top marketing firm, was thrilled. I remember she called me saying she couldn't wait to start working. Knowing she would be in a competitive industry, I tried to warn her to be ready for the personalities she would be dealing with. A couple of months after working there, she gave me a call. Her voice was different this time; her excitement had quickly turned to stress due to dealing with a toxic boss, Michael. He was demanding and demeaning, taking credit for his team's work and belittling them publicly. The constant anxiety affected Jessica's personal life and well-being.

Fed up after a particularly harsh meeting, Jessica told me she had taken action. She scheduled a one-on-one conversation with Michael, calmly outlining specific instances of his inappropriate behavior and its impact on her. She emphasized her dedication to the company while asserting her need for respect and a supportive work environment.

Surprisingly, Michael seemed taken aback and acknowledged he needed to adjust his approach. While the change was gradual, Jessica began to notice some improvement. She also started practicing self-care, leaving work at a reasonable hour, and not answering non-urgent emails after hours. She formed a support group with colleagues, sharing strategies for coping with the toxic environment.

Realizing the company's culture would stay the same, Jessica began job hunting and eventually found a position that valued employee well-being. The move brought her immense relief and excitement.

Jessica's story reminds us of the importance of boundary-setting and advocating for ourselves. It highlights how self-care and support networks can help us navigate toxic work environments and lead to more fulfilling opportunities. In Jessica's case, her parents had worked with her boundary-setting since childhood. Her upbringing beautifully transcended into adulthood, and she has always been a friend I admire for reminding me why boundary-setting matters from a young age to adulthood.

Teaching Children About Boundaries

Establishing boundaries in nurturing young minds starts with something other than handing them a rulebook on interacting with others. It begins with a silent course that teaches them how to do so in everyday decisions. Adults model behaviors from which the children take cues as to what is appropriate regarding their personal space and consent. They understand that children are not born understanding these concepts and use their natural curiosity about the world around them.

Children learn about boundaries from explicit teaching and observing the behaviors of those around them. As they watch others navigate their relationships and set boundaries, kids naturally start to understand the importance of personal space and the value of saying no when necessary. This observation and learning continue as they age, shaping their boundaries and teaching them to prioritize their well-being. This approach teaches through demonstration, making it more effective than verbal instructions in raising children.

Age-Appropriate Conversations

As children start to grasp the concept of boundaries, it's the perfect opportunity for open conversations articulating these observed behaviors. Through intentional discussions tailored to the child's developmental stage, caregivers can lay the foundation for the child's understanding of boundaries, fostering a sense of security and autonomy as they navigate their world. For the tender minds of young children, the topics are tangible, addressing issues of personal space, the right to say no to unwanted touch, and the necessity of asking before borrowing. These context-based discussions form the crux of relationship education and serve well as a primer for the more complex topics of later years. As the child grows, the dialogue deepens, delving into the realms of emotional and digital boundaries—an especially vital conversation in the age of technology. As the child learns—one step at a time—the all-encompassing nature of boundaries, armed with the language to understand and articulate them, to live in their world safely and respectfully.

Respecting Children's Boundaries

Teaching children about boundaries almost invariably involves one aux-iliary lesson: respecting the boundaries they set. This strategy is often conducted through day-to-day interactions between children and adults. Thus, when a child expresses an aversion to a friendly hug from a relative or a desire to be alone at a party, the adult's compliance with the stated limits strengthens the child's understanding of boundaries as a mutual process. When consistently shown, this respect instills in the child a deeply rooted sense of self-respect. In step with their notion, "You are in charge of how people treat you," they understand that their voice is meaningful, that their comfort is essential, and that their needs and wishes are to be respected—equipping them with lifelong values of agency and respect for themselves and others.

Empowering Children

After equipping young children with an understanding of and respect for boundaries, the next step in fostering child development in this aspect of their lives is empowering children to assert their limits confidently. This empowerment is not about suddenly giving children authority. Still, they gently develop their ability to listen to their instincts, sense when a line—physical, emotional, or digital—has been crossed, and confidently voice their discomfort with the situation or refusal of something. The tools required to empower children in this way are present not in the abstract but in the concrete aspects of ordinary life.

Through imaginative play sessions designed to empower children to as-sert their boundaries and open-hearted talks about how everyone's bound-aries are equally important, we provide the knowledge to teach them how relationships work confidently and respectfully. Wielding these tools with patience and sensitivity can help a child build the discipline of setting up boundaries in familiar and safe spaces so that the child can apply these behaviors to the more complex world outside their home. Such empowerment, tempered with patience and excellent care, will arm the child with self-respect and a compass that will guide them through socializing experiences that will become richer and more complex as children grow from toddlers to teenagers. When leading children through the haunted woods of setting up and respecting boundaries, you should rely on subtle lessons of observed behavior and straightforward dialog that allows them to empower their voice confidently. Doing so strengthens their inner soul and is the best you can do for their future.

Respecting Others' Boundaries: The Flip Side

By now, you are probably thinking, man, boundaries are just so complex. Well, they are, but by acknowledging and honoring boundaries, the setting allows you to respect yourself and others. They are learning a new dialect of a complex language. Human relations demand constant observations, allowing us to commit to the sacredness of each person's autonomy profoundly. In this tender appeal to your humanity, interactions manifest in social niceties and venture deep into mutual respect and understanding.

The first step in this delicate subject is to listen and understand. It means putting aside your thoughts and paying attention to what others say and feel. You can often discover someone else's boundaries in the subtle signals they unknowingly display. These cues might be as simple as looking away when a question gets too personal, a brief pause before they respond, or a slight shift in their body language. To truly respect others' boundaries, it's essential to understand them intellectually and pay close attention to the subtle signals they give off. Everyone's story and comfort level are unique, just like yours. So, take the time to tune in and recognize these individual differences.

Empathy in Boundary Respect

At the heart of boundary respect lies empathy, the bridge that connects our own experiences with the feelings of others. This empathy does not merely sympathize with the discomfort or needs of another but seeks to inhabit their perspective, to understand the world through their eyes. Through this deep understanding, we learn to navigate the space around their boundaries carefully. They allow us to recognize that these limits are not obstacles to be challenged but expressions of their need for safety, respect, and autonomy. Cultivating this empathy transforms our approach to boundaries from mere compliance to genuine care, fostering respectful and enriching interactions for all involved.

Consent and Permission

Integral to the ethos of boundary respect is the principle of consent, a concept that transcends the physical to encompass all forms of interaction. Seeking permission, entering personal space, sharing sensitive information, or engaging in emotional discussions becomes a cornerstone of respectful interaction. This practice, rooted in recognizing the other's autonomy, elevates engagement from assumption to agreement, from intrusion to invitation. It is a testament to the value we place on the agency of others, a clear signal that their comfort and preferences are paramount in the dynamics of our interaction. In this light, consent becomes not just a formality but a fundamental expression of respect and a key ingredient in cultivating trust.

Building Trust

In relationships, trust is the most powerful bond that connects people and makes their connection possible, though fragile. Trust is earned through respect and integrity and is built on others' respect for your boundaries. When you show that you respect someone's boundaries, trust between you is built. Trust is like the bedrock of any meaningful relationship—it forms the foundation for open, honest conversations and deep connections. Conversely, another person's acknowledgment of one's boundaries can and will serve as a foundation for solid and healthy relationships. Therefore, the central element bound with the art of respecting others' boundaries is relationships, which is a prevalent definition of the term. Relationships built to last, effective, and inevitably robust are established on respect for everyone's right to their own space and boundaries.

By ensuring that the boundaries each person has established for themselves are understood and respected, one also guarantees another vital relationship-building block: security. If people's limits and needs are known and honored, those people will feel safer in each other's company and free to be themselves. They will feel free to be themselves in the relationships and will, thus, be more likely to initiate honest and open conversations. Developing such relationships and respecting others' boundaries is a journey that helps one discover the reality of one's individuality. One can learn, however, that being separate from others and their needs does not make communication impossible but can make it possible in new and unexpected ways that can be incredibly heartfelt and profound.

In conclusion, this chapter emphasizes the critical role of respecting boundaries, both one's own and others', in healthy relationships. By practicing recognition, empathizing, requesting consent, and building trust, we ensure that our interactions with others are authentic and considerate. The analysis has to be in-depth and challenging, requiring you to be open-minded and conscientious. Remember to use these lessons as you move on to future chapters, as they will be just as essential in the coming personal and relational development stages.

Chapter Six

CHAPTER 5

THE FOUNDATION OF HEALTHY RELATIONSHIPS

Chapter 5 The Foundation of Healthy Relationships

Between heartbeats, there is a silent and subtle pause. Trust is a belief in another's reliability, truth, and abilities. It develops from sharing secrets in a dimly lit room, from the pressure of someone's hand, and from the gaze accompanied by the message, "I am here." Trust is shifty and sometimes challenging to achieve and maintain. Once the link promising safety is lost, intensive care must be paid for every moment.

Trust: The Cornerstone of Connection

Trust is not built by grand acts or sweeping promises. The strength of our character isn't just forged in the grand moments of life but in the everyday, quiet rhythm that forms the backdrop of our existence. Our consistent actions and daily choices shape who we are and how we navigate the world. It is the coffee brewed every morning without having to ask, the friend who was never late, and the ally who never left when needed. Consistency, molded with honesty, paves the foundation to which we can entrust our dreams and vulnerabilities. Trust is much like a garden; it requires patience, care, and the acknowledgment that it will take a while to grow.

It can be seen when two partners are assigned to work in the same business and decide to cooperate and have a joint report. The foundation and renewability of their relationship are grounded not in the task itself but by the consistent reliability and the pureness of their intention to work. They meet the assignment's demands, open up when the primary partner needs more input, and create grounds for eventual productive and everlasting cooperation.

Rebuilding Trust

When trust is shattered, it's like a fragile vase breaking into a thousand pieces, each shard carrying the weight of suffering, disappointment, and betrayal. Putting it all together feels impossible, like trying to mend something beyond repair. But with patience and care, focusing on each crack and crevice, we can start the painstaking process of reconstruction. It's about seeing the broken pieces not as irreparable damage but as opportunities to create something more substantial. Each becomes a testament to resilience, turning what was once broken into a masterpiece of healing and renewal.

Trust and Vulnerability

Vulnerability is opening yourself up to potential harm, and trust is tested and strengthened in the crucible of vulnerability. It is a leap of faith where we believe our genuine character will not be condemned or cast aside. This pattern of trust and vulnerability is as old as civilization itself. For example, when someone tells us about a tragic incident that happened in their life, it often invokes a desire to know them better. It is not the sad tale that causes the desire but the fact that the other person views us as worthy of sharing it with. It's vulnerability – a willingness to trust another person's compassion and wisdom. It is the foundation of solid and flexible relationships.

Signs You Can Trust Someone

Usually, when we decide whether to trust someone, we rely on intuitive and acquired signs. One of them is the transparency of a person. It's the ability to share your emotions and feelings without veiled purpose, the conviction that our secrecy is not a guarantee of safety. Consistency is another crucial indicator that is accessible to all. In a relationship, if something needs to be added there, it is very doubtful that there is trust. Of course, signs also include someone's behavior. For example, a good sign of faith is a partner's ability to express their feelings and behave steadily in the sense of being together and support. If that happens, they can be trusted – and then we can be convinced of this again and again.

Communication: The Bridge Between Minds

Communication within relationships is like the work of a skilled weaver, delicately crafting each pattern to reveal our inner designs, thoughts, and emotions. Through this intricate weaving, we bridge the gaps between us, connecting remote and separate islands of existence. Communication remains not only a tool for success in life but also the very essence of connection, a delicate and contingent 'thing' that requires much skill and finesse.

Active listening is a critical and crucial aspect of this skill set. It exceeds the mere silence of the other party. It requires their participation and immersion in the moment by passing and reaching out to the conditions that made the original message possible. In particular, such listening must seek to understand the message in full and the valence it represents in terms of how its phrases and messages resonate in everyday thought and emotions. Creating a dedicated, judgment-free space ensures the existence of a context from which genuine communication can grow and to which it becomes irrelevant whether it is received or validated or not. Possible examples of this process include two friends spending an evening underneath a starry night sky. Each message uttered would receive not a recollection or an expectation of the response that will greet it but a full and active memory, each expression of agreement offering a further strand to their conversation.

Dialogue on Expressing Needs

There is no failed dialogue between people if they fearlessly express each other's needs and expectations. On the one hand, being open and vulnerable in your conversations is essential, as well as sharing your thoughts and aspirations openly. But on the other hand, expressing your desires shouldn't be reckless; it should be a dialogue filled with meaning and purpose. Balancing expressing your needs and understanding your conversation partner's response is crucial in communication. Based on this principle, the expression of needs should be chosen wisely, like laying cobblestones on a bridge — with love, instruction, and insight into the other's opinion.

Dialogue on Communication Conflict

Disagreements are a natural part of human interaction, so it's essential to approach dialogue to resolve conflicts without overpowering the other person. Since respect and understanding of both parties are the basis of dialogue, individuals should be aware of the course of finding a compromise. To this end, disputes should not be perceived as combat but as informative communication that allows you to understand another person and the situation and gain experience. In just one moment of conversation, a person can utter a word that brings harmony to the home, as some words are irreplaceable in their power to heal.

Non-Verbal Communication

The words we speak are only a tiny part of the conversation. It is only the tip of the iceberg, formed by the interchange of impressions and perspectives reaching beneath our feelings and thoughts. Indeed, non-verbal communication entails the bulk of the exchange of our views, which happens in complete silence. Non-verbal language is peculiar to most living creatures on the planet. It involves gestures, mimics, and even the utterances of the body. One can read non-verbal communication relatively quickly since it conveys the meaning far more precisely than any words can.

For example, a warm touch on a hand may significantly reassure a person. Similarly, looking aside during a conversation means the speaker needs to be more confident and comfortable. Additionally, open hands without an item mean that the person speaking is sincere and reliable. Reading non-verbal cues is beneficial because it adds many more levels of meaning to the conversation that anyone can articulate. Such contributes to the enrichment of the process. Listening is entirely related to picking up non-verbal signals because this is when one may "hear" the conversation, not just listen. Our needs, emotions, and pressures – everything can be picked up and responded to in this manner. It provides a way to navigate the intricacies of human experience.

Mutual Respect: Valuing Each Other's Individuality

Mutual respect is the silken thread anchoring the quilt of relationships. Mutual respect is akin to admiring the complexity of the lives of others. It's about taking a deeper look beyond what's immediately visible and appreciating all the diverse elements that shape their identity. Rather than viewing differences as obstacles, it involves celebrating them as the unique characteristics that add richness and depth to our interactions. We have a uniqueness, even if we all aspire to the same values. Many opinions, preferences, and goals exist, but we can and should respect them all.

Respecting differences goes beyond mere tolerance—it's about honoring the diverse array of people and experiences that make up the human landscape. To respect difference and diversity is not to be in a state of admiring reverie; it is a call to nurture the differences around us actively. It is going on a journey and being able to take the shape of the world that's connected to philosophy and values. This task is difficult but simultaneously incredibly satisfying: communicating with a person with opposing views allows us to "earn" different perspectives. It gives us the ability to understand others. As we grow in our relationships, understanding doesn't necessarily mean we have to agree with them. Getting to this phase in our lives is an opportunity to attain mutual sympathy and thrive.

Supporting autonomy

When we're in a relationship where we can be ourselves while still supporting each other, it's like flying a kite together. Just like holding the string of a kite, we both have our freedom but stay connected. It's like watching the kite soar high in the sky, dancing freely with the wind. In relationships, the string is the support that one person gives to another, taking care of their independence and realizing their desire for something. Mutually given freedom and autonomy are solid relationship values, creating the medium they can develop.

Making sure both partners have an equal say and value in your relationship is like building a solid foundation for a temple of mutual respect. It's not just about being fair; it's about weaving your voices and choices into a beautiful tapestry of decision-making. Each thread matters, and no one should overshadow the other. It's like creating a harmonious blend where both of you contribute equally. In this world of equality, every voice is like a melody, and every opinion adds to the harmony of agreement. You don't force decisions; you reach them with understanding and respect. This approach transforms your relationship into a partnership where both of you are valued and honored.

Relationships find their true strength and beauty in the serene embrace of mutual respect, where understanding fills the spaces between us. In acknowledging differences, honoring boundaries, supporting autonomy, and pursuing equality, we discover the foundation and essence of deep, enduring connections. It is in this sacred space that individuality is not just respected but celebrated, where the unique contributions of each enrich the collective journey, adding depth and dimension to the human experience.

Empathy: Walking in Their Shoes

Empathy is a concept that often seems straightforward on the surface but hides vast complexity. To experience empathy, one must go beyond one's perspective and put oneself in the place of another. One must not only occupy the position of another as an outsider looking in but instead become a member of their shared emotional world. This experience is not characterized by physical movement but rather one where psychological boundaries become fluid. Mirroring this openness is the required vulnerability only reciprocated by the party we open ourselves to. Through this experience, we achieve a deeply personal connection in which we understand how another feels, support them emotionally, and sometimes learn to share in their positive experiences. This process is also what separates empathy from bringing someone's concerns into consideration, a more detached process where emotions are not as involved.

Empathy is crucial in a conflict scenario, acting as a guiding light for a resolution. In an instance where two parties disagree, empathy assumes the value of being a lighthouse for emotions and reason. Empathy towards those one is in conflict with requires walking in the other side's shoes and leaving one's preconceptions behind. This process is not attempting to change others or use an understanding to form a counterargument but rather one of pure reflection. As su h, conflict resolution turns less about the imposition of needs and more about synthesizing both sides' wisdom to compromise on a solution that retains respect towards all positions involved.

Delving into the depths of empathy isn't a one-time thing; it's a journey that requires consistent practice and dedication. One of the critical methods to cultivate this empathy is through active listening. It's more than just hearing words; it's about decoding the unspoken messages hidden between the lines, pauses, and even in the tone of voice. By truly resonating with what others are expressing, we create a profound connection that goes beyond words.

Another powerful tool is asking open-ended questions. These encourage people to express themselves fully, even delving into realms they might not have explored. Engaging in this way signals our willingness to understand and connect with the other person truly. At the heart of empathy lies acceptance – accepting others for who they are, with all their joys, sorrows, and complexities.

When we approach others with empathy, it shows love in its purest form, enriching both the giver and the receiver. Each person brings a unique piece to the empathy puzzle, enhancing the human connection. Empathy plays a role in the formation/creation and then expansion of relations and values that are composed of many relations visible in our lives. It de elops the bond formed by ties. This one may be small or big, like thread, rope, or nonexistent.

Empathy isn't just about our individual experiences; it has the power to heal and bridge the divides we face in society. Empathy is an antidote to the growing gaps between people in a world where extreme individualism is rising. Empathy brings us back to understanding the collective aspects of human life. Everyone has a similar range of emotions, feelings, and experiences that unite all of us. Empathy invites us to explore our personal connections and broader horizons. It challenges us to resist the temptation to oversimplify others' experiences based on race, religion, or lifestyle. Empathy allows us to understand different people and see the whole range of human emotions even if they being experienced look different. With every concerned question, empathy teaches us to learn from those who are furthest from us.

Navigating the path of empathy can be challenging, but the rewards are immense. Empathy enriches our relationships, nurturing them to blossom even amidst challenges. Empathy isn't just about understanding; it's about going the extra mile to connect with others' experiences and emotions. It holds the key to addressing the divisive issues afflicting modern society. Instead of driving us apart, empathy calls us to unite and stand by each other through thick and thin, supporting one another in good and bad times.

Supporting Growth: Encouraging Personal Development

Nurturing personal or shared growth within the complexity of human relationships resembles the art of tending a garden, where diverse flowers thrive harmoniously. When two plants grow together, they must support each other without overshadowing their partners' needs, extending branches but not poignantly. It means that a shared field of understanding and experience benefits mutual growth as long as this environment satisfies the individual and the connection's needs. However, this concept seems more straightforward in the world of flora since both plants making up a relationship are alone in their solo pursuits. How do these parallel desires benefit and grow in their shared space? Thus, the intertwining flowers ensure that each quest is respected and maintained in the rich connection environment, further enhancing it.

Individual and Mutual Growth

Like the branches of a tree stretch towards different directions, nurturing individual aspirations means appreciating that they are alone and outward, hungering for their space and light. However, like the branches share the same root, the shared environment between two separate beings must account for these individual works. They must be treasured because enriching individual quests will not overshadow the shared interest but nourish and enrich it, making the experience more profound. It is manifested through acts such as support towards pursuing the other's goals and ambitions and conversations that bring this quest to light. Finally, these too-solo assemblies should have the chance to celebrate their solo triumphs that ultimately enrich the experience of shared aspirations.

Encouragement vs. Pressure

Genuine encouragement is like a warm breeze, gently guiding and uplifting without overwhelming. But pressure can be as relentless as a raging storm, threatening to drown out the individual's rhythm. To truly understand the difference, you must listen closely to the other person's needs, knowing when to gently nudge, step back, and let them find their way. This approach creates a nurturing environment where growth unfolds naturally, like a vast field of wildflowers swaying in the breeze, each blooming at its own pace.

Celebrating Achievements

In our growth journey, recognizing our progress is like finding landmarks along a winding mountain trail. Each milestone, whether big or small, determines how far we've come and how much further we have to go. Just as mountain travelers find joy in reaching each peak or pass, we should celebrate our achievements, no matter how modest they seem. These celebrations don't have to be extravagant; even the smallest gestures of acknowledgment can be significant.

Learning Together

The willingness to take on new challenges and skills together is the foundation of the notion that relationships can never be fixed. Collecting experience together, two people walk a road into the unknown, expanding their horizons and those of a shared relationship. Learning together, thus, is not just about the acquisition of new skills or picking up new pieces of experience; instead, the process creates a crisis that, in turn, shapes a new relationship between two people.

Notably, the ways to learn together can range from accidental to premeditative, from taking a left turn on a bike down a new trail for the first time to a preplanned journey. At the same time, each new specimen of experience enhances solidarity between the two people, making the relationship more robust, flexible, and less prone to stress. Consequently, the more one learns with one's friend or significant other, the more united and mature the relationship gets, eventually turning it into a colossal experience of self-exploration and self-improvement.

Once the final step of the process has been taken, and two people learn something new together, it cannot be underestimated. At this point, the relationship is transformed into a particular dimension: helping and supporting each other and one's self-balancing each other out and feeding the relationship with unstoppable energy, constantly looking for new skills and challenges. It is important to remember that it is only in this unique dimension that two people can reveal the true power of the relationship between them.

Healthy Conflict Resolution: Finding Common Ground

Conflict doesn't happen from the outside; it's part and parcel of our relationships. When disputes arise, they show us how solid or fragile our connections are. While conflict might seem negative, it's a chance for us to dig deeper and understand each other better. It's like shining a light on the intricate workings of our relationships. Those willing to face conflict head-on often come out the other side with a deeper understanding and respect for each other. Amid conflict, negotiation, and compromise are the tools that help us find our way through. The need for the skillful use of communication tools in the framework of successful negotiation demands the delicate choice of the right ones, as different sets promote not different results but somewhat different themes that surround the discussion and compromise. The first, clinging to the safety and clarity of "I" statements, ensures that the most personal observations and requests will be made while not blaming the other side.

In that same safety and security environment, these conflicts can be seen as personal challenges and opportunities for growth. Instead of pointing fingers or blaming each other, it's about listening, understanding, and finding common ground. It's about leading by example, showing support and empathy, and asking questions to understand where the other person is coming from.

The main idea of the compromise is the possibility to honor the sides involved, thinking of the needs and boundaries of other people in which they can agree upon concepts created not to be excellent though; they may be just a combination of wrong decisions. It is similar to mixing different colors to make the third one when the first two are combined. The compromise can be regarded from the perspective of readiness to do wrong, which means that people are ready to return when required. It is impossible to compromise if a person is unwilling to return and remain in his position, as a compromise requires both sides to go back simultaneously.

When the storm of conflict passes, it leaves behind a changed landscape in the relationship, a reminder of its resilience. The real work begins at this point – rebuilding on the bedrock of understanding and respect. The focus now is on making sure both partners feel valued and heard, knowing that every perspective matters in the journey of the relationship. However, re-building does not occur through some grand efforts; instead, the experience of recognizing worth is in the simple but firm recognition of each other, the acknowledgment of pain and effort, and the joint commitment to a future based on ongoing discussion. As a result, by these means, following such a phase, the relationship does not weaken but instead grows stronger, having gone through conflict together.

Regarding the notion of healthy conflict resolution, it is possible to point out that this issue is touched upon in a landscape rich with the po-tential for growth, understanding, and a deeper connection. Conflict is not avoided as it can become an important trigger that stimulates exploration and evolution. At the same time, it is important not only in the process of conflict resolution but in "managing the aftermath." While challenging events may be tricky, they serve as catalysts for building and enriching relationships. These experiences have a multiplier effect, amplifying the benefits and outcomes beyond what might have been expected initially. Relationships would be balanced without conflicts, but it does not mean they would be solid and long-lasting. This desire to prove that bonds are strong enough to overcome anything and find a compromise to remain connected is a primary precondition for further development and a guar-antee that relationships will be long-lasting. In the end, healthy conflict resolution makes people learn more about each other as they become more understanding and connected.

Maintaining Individuality

Each person's individuality should be honored like a holy grove—a sanctuary where our deepest thoughts and feelings can be expressed and cherished, allowing our true selves to flourish. In the depths of our everyday pursuits and personal interests, in those moments of quiet reflection, we uncover the essence of who we are. It's not about withdrawing from the world; it's about embracing our individuality and celebrating the unique contributions we each bring to the table. Ensuring a deep connection with yourself is essential—it gives each of us a seat at the table in the grand structure of togetherness. It's like having a personal invitation to contribute your unique essence to the collective experience.

Healthy Separateness

As we indulge in being together through our shared experiences, dreams, and efforts, there's a beauty in the spaces of separation that encircle this seemingly seamless masterpiece. Just like the pauses between spoken words or the quiet moments in a piece of music, these spaces add depth and richness to the overall picture of love. Love isn't just about being constantly together or merging into one entity. It's about cherishing and valuing each other's individuality and unique perspectives. When we embrace our separateness and allow ourselves to explore our thoughts and experiences, we bring back treasures to share. It's like wandering through the vast fields of our minds and returning with handfuls of flowers to exchange with our loved ones.

The bedrock of this equilibrium is trust, a silent bond where freedom is granted with the promise of faith, not just in the fidelity of the body but of the heart and soul. In relationships, trust encompasses more than mere expectations of loyalty. Trust becomes the wind beneath the flesh-and-bone wings of independence. It guides you towards personal development and safety in the shared certainty of staying afloat together instead of treading in separate directions. However, such trust is not the result of ignorance and naivety. It is the fruit of overcoming challenges and exposing yourself, diving into the ocean of your partner's vulnerabilities. It creates a bond that remains firm, although based on trust. As paradoxical as it may sound, the balance between togetherness and freedom does not forbid the boundless sea before an individual.

A stable and healthy relationship is more of an art than a science. It has to be based on solid communication, making it perfect thanks to its simplicity. It includes the possible elements of togetherness and independence and purges the mixture, turning the two into a combination that is the right proportion. It involves compromise but is not limited to formal equality. If togetherness becomes more than independence, little room is left for development; conversely, if the relationship is based solely on divided independence, there is little difference between two separate entities. With independence as the underlying premise, individuals can share experiences that can be embraced. Individuality is the gift that the union of the "self" and the "other" yields.

Recognizing Healthy vs. Unhealthy Jealousy

In the multifaceted sphere of human relations, jealousy is often like a gate crasher, casting doubts and shadows in the space of intimacy and connection between individuals. This age-old emotion passes through four stages of jealousy in any relationship, varying from the slightest tint of unease to the darkest hues of torment. It is paramount to come to terms with the idea that a streak of jealousy can sometimes be interwoven into the structure of a relationship without undermining its durability.

Sometimes, it might echo tenderness and dedication to a person or a friend that has entered your life, coupled with the fear of losing them. Nevertheless, the thin line between a bit of jealousy that can give a relationship a shade of joy and a corrosive acidic liquid that destroys can be hard to distinguish. Indeed, if debarred from defining these two emotions as one pair of side-by-side regards, it is hard to tell whether the subsequent feelings and outcomes emerge from jealousy.

When you feel jealousy, adding a comforting reassurance of understanding has the power to breathe new life into a relationship. A dialogue on vulnerability and the hidden insecurities that govern your encompassing self brings jealousy under control. It emasculates it to an insignificant iota of self that needs development.

Communication about Jealousy

When the heart pounds with the weight of unspoken fears, it takes a courageous leap into the unknown, facing what scares us most. In that moment, fear transforms from a barrier into a bridge, connecting us to new possibilities. Our hearts become intertwined in communication, forging connections that bind us together. Words become bridges, spanning the distance between us. Empathy is the fertile ground where understanding takes root within the delicate balance of conversation. Our words are not merely a chaotic clash of bold actions, a flurry of demands and justifications. Instead, they carry a plea, a call for understanding and connection. These voices blend through dialogue, ensuring we form a bond rather than drift apart.

Jealousy's Root Causes

What causes jealousy? It often originates from deep-seated fears and insecurities. It may usually come from how we view ourselves and our self-worth, causing us to think there are threats to our relationships. Maybe those feeling intense jealousy have experienced betrayal. This emotion can just be influenced by many factors: our upbringing, past relationships, and our insecurities. To move forward, we must dig deep into the bottom of our emotions and understand what nourishes jealousy.

Managing Jealousy

The management of jealousy, a task as complex as the emotion itself, unfolds across a landscape marked by personal growth and relational understanding. Strategies to navigate this area of our lives are as varied as those who experience them. We all share a common thread—the quest for equilibrium between trust in the self and faith in the other. This equilibrium is nurtured through practices that anchor the self in the bedrock of self-esteem and mutual respect, cultivate open dialogues that bridge a misunderstanding, and deliberately reinforce the bonds that bring us together. In the end, jealousy, when met with the embrace of understanding and the warmth of assurance, can become not what destroys the relationship but what enriches its depth and complexity.

The Role of Intimacy: Connecting Beyond the Physical

Human connection has nothing more vital and nothing more powerful than intimacy. It meanders through the core of our relationships, intertwining us in a mesh of shared experiences, vulnerabilities, and truths. It transcends the physical, seeping into the emotional, intellectual, and spiritual heart of our connections, where the roots of our closeness lie and bloom. Intimacy is so powerful; it is a discreet yet powerful understanding between friends or partners. It is the simple act of being with another person, sharing one's fears and unspoken dreams, and having a setting where you can say more than a thousand words just by looking at each other. It is sensual, tender, and infinitely comforting, and the knowledge that you and another person share this type of closeness creates an understanding of incredible depth.

Forms of Intimacy

I wanted to explore a few other concepts of intimacy; however, I want to ensure that you have a better understanding of the human heart. Emotional intimacy, through its root form, can be seen as "human intimacy," a profound closeness that connects people on the deepest subconscious levels. At the same time, intellectual intimacy involves the closeness between two partners in an argument or discussion. The profound, satisfying consistency of understanding emerges when two minds meet and begin to agree. Spiritual intimacy, ultimately, brings people together through an experience and shared beliefs and values when two souls meet and, in doing so, discern. It is a true sense of shared purpose, shared faith, and shared understanding of the importance of the tangible world.

Building Emotional Intimacy

The foundation of emotional intimacy is laid in sharing vulnerabilities, an act as brave as it is tender. This sharing, a gradual unpeeling of the self, calls for a mutual vulnerability that could create stronger bonds than steel. It is in the telling of one's fears, the admitting of one's dreams, and the sharing of one's hopes that we can experience a closeness untouched by the scorching rays of the masks we are required to wear to traverse our daily existence. Though rife with the danger of rejection, this journey towards intimacy offers a reward that is second to none. A profound, reverberating relationship that thrives on an offshoot of its roots into the land of authenticity and mutual acceptance. To develop emotional intimacy is to metaphorically construct a bridge across the abyss of isolation, on which the bricks of shared truths are set in the mortar of mutual compassion.

Maintaining Intimacy

The upkeep of intimacy, as crucial as its development phase, is a process in which the channels of open communication and shared experiences must be continually reupholstered. Open communication, the bloodstream of intimacy, ensures that the passageways between the hearts stay open and transparent, unclouded by the bushes of unspoken grievances and misunderstanding. Shared experiences are like the sturdy bridges that connect us, connecting memories into the very core of our relationships. Each moment we spend together becomes a cornerstone filled with laughter, tears, and the thrill of discovery. In maintaining these aspects, the age-old existence of intimacy is not only conserved but promoted, allowing its roots to grow deeper.

Of course, despite how wonderful and rewarding the path of intimacy is, it does not go without its challenges. The first challenge that often arises is stress, that ever-looming shadow that accompanies the daily life of any couple. When both partners are overwhelmed, stress can swiftly build walls between their hearts, hindering their connection. When two people are overwhelmed, it is easy for stress to erect barriers between the two hearts, obstructing their closeness. Similarly, the couple's history of past traumas may remain in their memories and manifest as barriers to their vulnerability. The second issue is awareness – an obstacle that requires vigilance that forces two people who choose a path of intimacy to face all the threats and pitfalls that such a path may bring. Through awareness, mutual understanding, and support, two people either come closer together, re-enforced by the crash of life's waves or remain at a distance, shattered by the same obstacles that maintained their bond.

As people address issues, intimacy flourishes and shows its true colors. In properly handling times of stress, addressing the sources of stress with a gentle touch, and confronting the issues that arise with the awareness of the roots of each, every couple discovers the strength of their bonds. It passes yet another intimate test, becoming closer than before. Indeed, in the whirlwind of humanity, intimacy serves as an oasis in which the proper form of connection between people is expressed and tested – and only the most durable and tender love may survive the tests during a relationship.

Consistency: The Quiet Assurance of Stability

Consistency is the silent sentinel of enduring relationships. As with most things eternal, it usually goes unnoticed but is strongly felt. Consistency is the bedrock of any connection and is inherently intertwined with repeating one's actions or behaviors. It ensures a partner's care is tangible, and your support can be relied upon. A relationship built on solidarity and consistency is one where a shared set of values underpin the partnership.

Consistency is not an act but a habit. It is the norm against which healthy relationships are measured, with a set rhythm and pattern. Therefore, consistency's role is much like a heartbeat, a recurring melody that speaks of the safety of a loving embrace. The connection between predictability and spontaneity can best be described as a seamless dance between you and the other person. Unfortunately, predictability can also hardly be considered to be drudgery if it incorporates reality's occasionally spontaneous surprises, whether they are positive or not. Predictability becomes the unshakable foundation, and spontaneity becomes the unpredictability of life. The important thing here is that life will happen, and as long as you have that consistency in it, you will be okay.

When the feeling of uncertainty creeps into a relationship, it's like sailing through dense fog without a compass. The inconsistency and unpredictability of one partner can feel like being tossed in a storm with no clear path forward. In such moments, trust becomes fragile, and stability and reliability are paramount. The first step in understanding this phenomenon is its impact on our relationships. It's like realizing the full force of a storm and how it can rock the boat of our connection. Once we understand this, we can navigate back to calmer waters by rediscovering the core of our relationship that the storm disrupted.

It's fascinating how people can change. Emotions can be like wild storms, intense and unpredictable, yet they also have a way of calming down, just like waves settling under the warm embrace of the sun. Therefore, to create a firm and stable stone of daily practices, words, and actions and run a spark of emotional support along it, developing qualities that soften the subtle vibrations of a changeable life is necessary. Building the right relationships demands keen awareness and vigilance in navigating the ebb and flow of interactions. Continuous communication, mutual understanding, transparent acceptance, and upkeep are the primary nurturers in fostering the growth of conducive environments and tools for genuine relationships to flourish. These elements lay the foundation for a robust intertwining of nurturing, evolving, and supportive bonds.

After this brief exploration of consistency, one thing becomes clear. The strength of relationships does not lie in the extraordinary actions or exuberant declarations of love, which can decay and dissipate shortly after they appear, but in the quiet reliability and stability that consistency provides. With every action done with goodwill and a desire to care and to help, the meaning of any relationship becomes more and more resilient. By maintaining the precarious balance of being just predictable enough and unpredictable enough, it withstands the hurricanes of doubt and the erosion of trust they bring. By steadfastly charting your course through the unexpected world of human relationships, you lay a stable foundation for the garden of connections to flourish. Please continue your journey with the understanding that, however quiet and unassuming, the power of consistency still allows relationships to prevail, forming a solid, sturdy baseline for their healthy and vibrant development.

Chapter Seven

CHAPTER 6

Navigating New Beginnings After Toxicity

A
s you enter a new relationship, especially after undergoing past toxic experiences with others, it could feel like finally emerging from deep waters and taking a long, refreshing breath. It is like inhaling crisp, cool air and seeing everything with newfound clarity. It brings immense relief, but at the same time, there may be a lingering worry about the possibility of diving back into the same situation. Experiencing these emotions demands readiness and a profound reflection on timing and approach. You have to carefully consider how and when to invite this new person into a space that you have cleansed and cleared of past toxicity.

When to Start Dating Again: Assessing Your Readiness

Evaluating the emotional status after a toxic relationship is like checking the garden after the storm – understanding what is left off, what needs to be thrown away, and that everything will grow back. The best way to deal with it is by being mindful and spending a weekend in your own space, putting feelings about dating into a journal. It would help if you were as sincere as possible with yourself and came to terms with the fact that someone in the past hurt you. Realize that the people you meet in the future may not be like that. For some people, it might be that the thought or idea of a person's company does not make them fearful anymore but careful instead.

Learning from Past Relationships

Lessons from a past toxic relationship can be compared to going through the same path but having a map this time. It is all about recognizing dangerous patterns, knowing what boundaries were crossed, and realizing the warning signs that have been missed. Such learning can be seen when talking with a trusted friend in a safe place. A small coffee shop far from the big city would be the most suitable place for such conversations, where people are not in a hurry and cannot be distracted.

Signs of Readiness

The first indicator of readiness is emotional stability. Self-confidence and the ability to set boundaries for others are the main signs. In real life, they will manifest themselves in different ways. If you have not done this for a long time, you can relax with yourself, make decisions without harming yourself, and not worry about the things that used to excite you. Then, you may also enjoy watching a movie with yourself and consider this evening a good use. Learn to love yourself and enjoy your own company.

Taking It Slow

The crucial importance of not rushing into a new relationship cannot be exaggerated. It's almost as if you are learning to walk after breaking a leg. Every new step is taken with circumspection and observation. Applying this concept to new connections will mean letting things take their course naturally, unburdened with deadlines and expectations. It can be turned into a practical instruction of composing and writing down some personal rules for dating. For instance, only introduce a new partner to family or close friends after gaining solid knowledge and trust. Sometimes, doing things at a slow pace can come a long way.

Visual Element: The Healing Garden Infographic

Picture yourself strolling through a serene garden, surrounded by the beauty of nature. As you walk, you reflect on your past relationships and how they've shaped you. The Healing Garden infographic is like your guide through this emotional journey. It's there to help you navigate the struggles of healing from past hurts and decide when to open your heart again. At the center of it all is a cozy nest, a reminder to take care of yourself and nurture your inner strength before venturing into new relationships.

As spring progresses, the garden becomes a lush oasis of personal development. Each new bloom symbolizes a milestone in readiness for new connections, from embracing solitude to asserting healthy boundaries. Just like a garden needs time to flourish, the heart also requires nurturing and patience before venturing into new relationships.

More than anything, this visual creation is a perfect reminder that nothing worthwhile comes easy. Healing and being ready for new connections is a matter of patience and perseverance, no less than a sobering journey. A change in approach does not mean moving the past under the carpet but integrating it and its lessons into our future ventures. We will proceed cautiously in our subsequent relationships. However, cautiously does not mean pessimistically.

Instead, it means taking our future partners' characteristics, needs, and personal permissions much more into account. The readiness to date once more thus becomes not just a step but also a testimony to our adaptability, an assertion that we have emerged from adversity as better versions of ourselves.

Red Flags and Green Flags: Knowing What to Look For

As we explore new relationships, It's crucial to spot warning signs like red and green flags to chart a safe course. Each red and green flag serves as a guide, directing our decisions and movements in the intricate dance of human interaction.

Identifying Red Flags

Within relationships, biases appear as subtle hints that are easily missed but crucial to catch. It's like a feeling that something is not quite right. Your intuition may be telling you to look further. Biases sneak into our conversations, our actions, and even our body language—tiny clues that can stir up a sense of unease. Sometimes, we brush them off as nothing, just a passing annoyance. But other times, the more you pay attention, everything eventually makes sense.

Recognizing Green Flags

In contrast, each green flag lights the way with the promise of potential, collectively representing a healthy partnership where both parties are respectful and kind to each other and where boundaries are consistently respected. It also means that a partner is empathetic and understanding and communicates their feelings and thoughts openly and honestly. Green flags in any relationship require more than just realizing they are present in a connection; they demonstrate the adage, "To know me is to love me." To truly realize that your partner's survival, water, nourishment, and growth are based on the need to understand that you need to be each other's shared oases. It would help if you appreciate these signs of a healthy connection.

Each green flag is based on your commitment to the relationship, carrying each other forward through life.

Trusting Your Instincts

Remember that the echoes of past experiences can sometimes drown out the whispers of intuition as we step into new relationships. Trusting one's instincts, however, and understanding whether there are red or green flags requires a conscious effort to quiet the noise and listen to the subtle stirrings of our gut – comfort or caution. In every twitch of doubt and every tranquil surge of comfort, instincts murmur truths that, when finally listened to, guide our path toward the connections ringing with the harmonious hum of well-being and mutual respect.

Seeking Balance

Navigating a new relationship is like exploring uncharted terrain, where finding the right balance between caution and optimism is extremely important. Relationships built on this balance are founded on mutual support, respect, and similar goals and aspirations. They require an alchemy of patience and hope, balance and uniting cautions and openness. Every new relationship follows a path from the scars of warning signs to the greener light of newly blooming connections. Every step you take should be developing a new relationship and attempting to find new connections built on mutual respect, trust, and understanding.

The key to this balance lies in awareness of red and green flags, warning signals, and pleasant surprises. Red flags signal a memory that you would never again want to experience. They are the scars that you would like to avoid and the motivation that drives you to find a supportive and uplifting relationship. They are the past connections that cannot be repeated in the present or future. A red flag isn't just a warning sign; it's the feeling in your core that cautions you from past experiences. They add depth to the foundation upon which new bonds of respect and trust are formed. For you to prevent the ghosts of the past from haunting the present, it's essential to integrate those experiences into the journey toward complete healing and recovery.

The Importance of Transparency: Sharing Your Past

Navigating the complexities of sharing your past—what to reveal, when, and how much—is akin to solving an intricate puzzle. It's all within threads of vulnerability, caution, and a longing for trust. Each piece you choose to disclose adds another layer to the puzzle, revealing more of yourself to the other person. As you go through this journey, you unfold and share your past and the stories that can help others know more about you.

Navigating the terrain of honoring each other's pasts is akin to wandering through a hall of mirrors. Some reflections gleam brightly in the light, while others lurk in shadowy corners, haunted by the specters of past relationships. Embracing these reflections requires a willingness to accept them, knowing that they can open another's heart to scrutiny. Walking through each other's pasts is like carefully walking through another person's footsteps, knowing where reservations may lie and where they rejoice. It is also the authorship of the truth, regardless of its neutral or red testament. Thus, respecting each other's sigils or dismissing them is a matter of the constellations of each other's connections, cut or woven to the tastes of the other.

Respecting each other's pasts is akin to navigating a path marked by healthy boundaries, much like the unspoken signals that guide us along the easiest route. Just as a boundary silently implies the need to stay clear of certain areas, so does honoring each other's pasts, signaling the importance of treading carefully and respectfully. For all those things, a stray gentle push is the sign of all things uncommunicated, both the spoken and unspoken rules by which former lovers with new faces use to stay friends.

In the tender and confidential exchange of our pasts, our relationship blossomed with openness and clarity, creating a space where we could truly understand each other. In our moments of dialogue, honesty, and observance of one another's limits in relationships, there and then, the future is being built from the past. In that future, the past is not a ghost but a collective symbol from other times, which lights the way to a more promising present and future.

Building Trust: A Gradual Process

Building trust is a journey that unfolds over time, not merely through the quantity of interactions but rather the quality and depth of those connections. As a result, trust is not a single monolithic phenomenon; instead, it is a mosaic, a collection of shared experiences, promises kept, vulnerabilities shared, and forgotten secrets kept in the essence of mutual respect.

Steps to Building Trust

Trust is constructed piece by piece, with each action contributing to the sturdy foundation upon which it rests. Though individual actions may seem insignificant on their own, they form an unshakable structure of trust when accumulated over time. Every action, whether answering a phone call promptly or offering support in times of need, reflects a desire to do good for others. No matter how small, each gesture is a building block in building trust. The small things matter, such as the willingness to make others' lives easier without loud announcements. The ears that listen, the arms that hug, and the voice that makes you feel better about yourself build trust. Each action must be wrapped in a deliberate meaning, for it would only be possible to gain confidence with carefully orchestrated, insincere displays.

Rebuilding Trust After Betrayal

When trust is shattered, piecing it back together can feel like trying to mend a broken vase—it takes time, care, and a steady hand. Taking responsibility for the mistake and actively working to rebuild trust is like carefully arranging the shards, hoping they fit back together seamlessly. Yet, with each tentative step forward, there's often a setback, a stumble that threatens to undo progress. It's a slow, painstaking process marked by moments of doubt, fear, and frustration. But with patience and perseverance, trust can gradually retake root, finding its place amid the wreckage. It's in the struggle and the effort, in the willingness to confront the pain head-on, that trust has the opportunity to grow anew.

Trust and Vulnerability

The core of trust is a precious stone of vulnerability, with its edges shining with the light of real ties. Offering your vulnerabilities to someone is brave, and deciding to put your heart and soul on the pitch with the sureness that a fall does not mean doom. Such an exchange of vulnerabilities acts pluses into the piggy bank of trust, and they become the currency for both sides. Taking the risk of vulnerability gives others value. As we expose our vulnerability to others, we offer weaknesses not for discrimination but for pleasant judgment. The power of such a connection is refractive and depends on the sincerity and security of the relationship.

Patience and Persistence

Building trust is not a time-bound phenomenon. Instead, it evolves with the accumulation of experiences rather than the passage of time. Therefore, this progression may take longer to tolerate, but it is necessary since it is the only way to build profound and sustainable trust. Consequently, patience becomes a virtue and a method to achieve the desirable state. At the same time, this patience must be combined with a kind of persistence that can be described as "stubborn." In other words, it is crucial to accumulate experiences without being discouraged by the obstacles and mistakes that can be expected to accompany the process. In this way, they become a part of the overall accumulation of actions proving loyalty and trust that, in turn, can develop trust in the relationship.

Avoiding Rebound Relationships: The Trap of Immediate Comfort

The breakup of toxic relationships leave people with alot of emotions. Rebound relationships may appear as a safe harbor, promising comfort after a breakup. However, this illusion of safety can quickly reveal itself as problematic. What initially seems like a white sandy beach can be treacherous rocks. Thus, it highlights the issue of recognizing when a person is tempted with a seemingly safe harbor and understanding why rebound relationships seem so attractively paradoxical.

Recognizing Rebound Situations

Recognizing a rebound scenario requires a certain level of self-awareness, self-confrontation, and internal contemplation. It is similar to looking in a mirror, not to admire yourself but to find the invisible signs of battle fatigue left by the skirmishes that took place. This process involves the assessment of one's inner motivation and marking the need to find a meaning of closeness in someone's vicinity or the necessity to hide from solitude. It needs to be arranged as a break, a reprieve on the way, a delay in the regress movement, not a trip towards some distant goal that anyone may set for themselves.

Emotional Unavailability

In rebound relationships, this lingering feeling is almost like an emptiness—the struggle with emotional unavailability. You can't point to it but can sense it in awkward silence or when conversations stay shallow. Emotional unavailability often comes from past pain, making it hard to open up and connect with someone new. It's not a choice but a defense mechanism to protect yourself from getting hurt again. However, recognizing this struggle is the first step in breaking free from the cycle, and it is essential to understand that healing has to start from within, not from someone else.

Taking Time to Heal

Allowing yourself the space and time to heal is a testament to the complexity of human emotions. It's acknowledging that your heart's wounds can't be rushed to closure by diving into new relationships; instead, they require the gentle exploration of self-discovery and inner peace. Grieving isn't a pause in life; it's a deepening of your experience and a form of self-care. Self-recovery embodies self-love and the deliberate decision to go through the trials that life throws at us. Taking time to heal is about reconnecting with yourself, learning what brings you fulfillment, and cherishing the quiet moments of solitude that resonate with your soul.

Signs of a Healthy New Relationship

The dawn of a healthy new relationship, emerging from the shadows of a toxic past or the emptiness of a rebound, feels like rain falling on parched soil. A healthy new relationship feels like finding solid ground after stumbling through quicksand. It's like discovering an oasis in the desert after wandering lost for so long. There's a warmth and comfort in knowing that you're with someone who genuinely cares about you and respects you for who you are.

The signs of a healthy relationship appear in the quality of interaction and the texture of communication: no hurry, no secrets, no poisons, only life and interactions. It is marked by the balance of support, not giving away crumbs out of fear of scarcity, but equally present in giving and taking. In the heart of a healthy new relationship, what truly stands out is the genuine presence of the other person. It's not about filling a void or fulfilling a need within ourselves, but rather about embracing the other person as their unique being. It's a connection beyond physical attraction or convenience; it's about truly seeing and appreciating each other for who we are, flaws and all.

In contrast, the threads of rebound relationships are often faced with immediate comfort or the allure of a fresh start. They're overshadowed by the looming gap left by the absence of genuine connection. Ultimately, they're destined to unravel abruptly, leaving behind nothing but emptiness. The way out of their enemy bonds and the way to the land of the abundance of beautiful relationships is a pilgrimage into yourself, an exodus into the answers promised by solitude, planting the seeds of "me" to harvest "us."

The Role of Self-Love in Attracting Healthy Relationships

Once you've left the toxic relationship, there's a sacred time that should be your time to heal—healing every single inch of pain and nurturing yourself with love matters. Why? Because then, you also allow the space needed for new connections to bloom and grow. This self-love, often a distant concept rather than a tangible practice in our healing journey, goes beyond the trendy self-care routines. It's about something more profound, a fundamental truth. The depth of our relationships mirrors the value and worth we attribute to ourselves as specific as the laws of attraction themselves: like attracts like. So, when a heart is nurtured in the warmth of self-love, it naturally gravitates towards those who resonate with that same sense of self-worth and acceptance.

Self-Love as the Foundation

Self-love is the nature of recognition of self-worth, the right to be happy, respected, and realized. It is that source of light that allows us not to drown in the darkness of doubts about ourselves and others. This light directs us to communicate in a place where our partner is not afraid of our fears but is attracted and inspired by our aura. But the brightness of this light is sustained only by the sincerity of this self-love, by the depths and inviolability of our commitment to it. Respecting your emotions, habits, and connections will allow you to protect yourself from the memories of past wounds. Such respect will also allow you to limit your self-perception.

Self-Work Before Partnership

Putting your well-being first goes a long way. It enables you to give yourself wholly when you enter a new relationship. It allows you to grow, learn, and love yourself unconditionally. As Lovelace stated, " You must be whole alone before you can truly complement another" (Lovelace, 2001). This statement serves as an epitome of the incredible power of self-work. Take the opportunity to take a cold-blooded look at yourself, which overlaps with your desires and frantic racing. From this self-work emerges a new self — one not weighed down by scars but by the armor you've been able to build as you face daily challenges. As you work on yourself, follow your path and resonate with your emotions, be intuitive with the world around you, and understand why loving yourself matters.

Attracting Like-Minded Partners

Meeting others who share your values, aspirations, and self-esteem feels like discovering a magical connection, where resonance becomes the guiding force, one that guides the relationship. Our highest frequency of self-love is pulling others towards us, extending towards people with similar levels of self-regard. It's not about being a passive recipient of fate but about radiating your authentic self and broadcasting your value into the world. Knowing who you are, your core values and the journey you want to embark on keeps you focused. When you've worked on yourself for the better, your subconscious and the inner you will even realize if that match with someone else is there. This intuition can come up while connecting with others, whether in your work environment, family, friends, or romantic relationships. Eventually, you realize that some people are at a different level of connection than you'd like them to be on.

Self-Love Practices

Everyday practice of self-love focused on rituals and routines towards your inner flame is the best act you can do for yourself. At the heart of this is the achievement of self-worth and building walls that cannot be torn down. For some, it might be practice in the form of exercise, working on a project, or creating time aside for personal self-care like baths, facials, and massages. However, the most fierce and constant practice of self-love is the cultivation of solitude as a sacred space around you and within you. Here, you can be with yourself, your thoughts, your dreams, and your desires, and you do not need to be drowned by others. Here, you can learn your own heart's language, which is unique to you, yet share many universal words across the distance, a language of love and wanting to be loved and connected. Thus, self-love is composed of the cycle of becoming and practicing it, and it is both the first ring and the last higher on the spiral path of your journey toward attracting healthy relationships.

Healing Together: When Both Partners Have Toxic Pasts

Unfortunately, this can be more common than you think. Again, it is often seen how people jump into relationships. As soon as the sadness of a past relationship passes, many believe they are ready, but as you've seen throughout the book, sometimes there's just a little more to unfold. In this case, two individuals are torn. Such causes emotional baggage, unresolved issues, and a lack of trust to be introduced in their new relationships. Coming in with baggage can cause frequent conflicts, lack of communication, and an uncomfortable feeling for both. People come in with toxic behaviors and lack a commitment to their growth and readiness to address past traumas. The resistance to getting better can often cause a lack of relationship fulfillment.

Shared Healing

The first thing that comes to mind about the relationship between two people with toxic pasts is carelessness. A lack of care for themselves and others. Sounds rough, doesn't it? But let's face it, when have you seen a relationship thrive when so much emotional baggage is involved? Relationships in this situation are so fragile that even if growth is amidst, it can easily be destroyed by the slightest mistake or uncarefulness.

On the contrary, when two people connect and genuinely are willing to move forward, they share a space of healing and acknowledge the stories of each other's scars; it is unique. You understand that no healing is ever finite and that the journey never ends as long as both partners are by each other's side. The most beautiful thing about such a journey is that it turns past pain into the most inspiring source of strength. A new bond is formed when you present your wound and hear their struggles. Such comprised of every story and shared and pain unveils the brightest hope for the future.

Open Communication

Communication is key to fostering a relationship premised on two people with a past in toxic relationships. Having open communication requires you to lower your shields and let go of being too on edge. It allows you to be fully immersed and willing to share your fears, triggers, and insecurities. This form of communication is risky because it involves exposing your heart to potential pain, but this very risk makes the act of sharing powerful. As you exchange your truths genuinely without any fake fakeness, it is possible to come to a new level of understanding. Through a genuine manner, you can be uniquely empathetic and pave the way for understanding, trust, and an unbreakable connection between you and others. It requires authentic listening to understand and confidence in communicating your feelings without being judged by the past. In such relationships, communication becomes the bridge to traverse troubled waters, and this is precisely the context that allows for the healing act of connection.

Supporting Each Other

It can be daunting as you are healing while supporting your partner. You might feel the temptation to fall into old habits. The bond forged between two people with a toxic past is a testament to their mutual understanding that healing is an individual journey. They recognize that no one else can walk that path for them, but they can offer support and companionship along the way. Balancing means allowing your partner to navigate their path of healing. It's about providing a gentle touch that acknowledges their pain without trying to fix it, being present in a way that speaks volumes of support without saying a word, and exercising patience without rushing them forward. Caring means understanding that love often resides in the

middle ground between allowing them without thinking about their healing journey and abandoning them at the first sign of trouble. It is the belief
in the strength of the other with a subtle touch of hope and the acceptance
that distance is sometimes needed for a person to regain their pace.

Setting Boundaries

By now, you've read a whole chapter on boundaries, and I can't emphasize
their importance. We previously described them as wall settings to protect
yourself. However, when you have chosen to be on the path with someone
who also has a toxic past, you are probably going to give that relationship
your all. Putting up walls towards that person might not help as you are
both healing together. In this sense, you can begin to look at boundaries
as landmarks. These are landmarks, markers that respect the needs of the
individuals, their specific paths of healing, and the baggage or triggers they
carry. Negotiating boundaries, viewed through mutual respect, is essentially an unspoken pact recognizing that each partner's healing journey
deserves space and autonomy. It is an understanding that the journey is
shared, but methods, speed, and commitment are different. In recognizing
these approaches to healing trauma, a relationship shifts from a place of
refuge to a home, the safe space that nurtures the healing, a bastion of
nurturing acceptance that does not serve to build distance but to foster
closeness.

As you walk hand in hand through your healing process, confronting
your scars and triggers together will allow your relationship to transform.
Knowing that you aren't alone in your journey is fantastic. It makes everything perfect when both partners understand that healing is their end
goal and can work towards the same thing. It evolves into a testament to
the potential for profound bonds, depth, and companionship even after
experiencing trauma. The new understanding of love carries baggage but
is a reminder of how battles were won, how resilience was tested, and how

hope was found and reignited.

Creating a New Narrative: Your Relationship, Your Rules

As you approach life with the openness to build new relationships after enduring a harsh, toxic past, it has to feel like you are embarking on a new chapter. It might feel like you are finally finding the courage to explore the unknown, knowing that the past doesn't define the future. This journey isn't just about finding someone new; it's about discovering yourself again, learning from past experiences, and setting healthier boundaries. It's about embracing vulnerability while being cautious, allowing yourself to love and be loved in a genuine and fulfilling way. As you embark on a new journey, it has to be about rewriting the story of love and relationships, painting a picture of trust, respect, and mutual growth.

Breaking Old Patterns

As you learn to recognize the patterns that no longer serve your best interests, it is a breakthrough moment, precisely when you realize they need to go. Knowing how to deal with and get past old habits is essential as they creep back into your life. Removing old patterns will require differentiation between what nurtures and what depletes. This discernment occurs through contemplation by scanning how your relationships have been going and finding the spots where they were diverging. Such requires you to be honest with yourself. Once you are, you can stand on the edge of choice, prepared to step into the patterns of behavior that validate your worth, respect, and boundaries and encourage growth. It is a conscious decision to step away from familiar behaviors and strive toward the unfamiliar, where the potential to forge genuine relationships based on mutual respect lies.

Establishing New Norms

Building the norms of a relationship isn't about following a societal blueprint; it's about creating something unique from your shared values, desires, and dreams. This co-creation is full of potential, where both voices carry equal weight, and the outcome is a shared vision of what your relationship can be. The relationship needs an open, judgment-free conversation atmosphere for this to work. You should feel free to express your desires and find compromises, understanding that relationships are living, evolving entities. Norms aren't rigid rules set in stone; they're flexible agreements that can grow and adapt as you both do. They are guidelines that keep the relationship steady by allowing flexibility when things are unplanned.

The Power of Co-Creation

Why is the power of a relationship created mutually? Because it comes from the shared experiences of both people involved. When two people come together to build their own story, it adds meaning and purpose to each of their lives. It's about autonomy, respect, and the mutual desire to create something unique, all woven into a surprisingly solid and flexible bond. Creating a relationship together becomes dynamic and full of life, reflecting the energy and effort you both put in. This mutual creation helps you break free from the past and any unhealthy patterns, allowing a new, respectful partnership to grow from the ashes. The real power of a mutually created relationship is the belief that you can build something far more significant than just a life for two. It becomes a thriving, enriching space where both partners can grow and support each other, creating something unique.

Leaving the Past Behind

Committing not to let past relationships affect your new ones is crucial, and it's not easy. It's about being firm yet gentle with yourself. As you find a support group or a partner, you must be open. Sometimes, making a promise with your partner or others not to let the past hurt can work as it protects your new beginning. Such allows you to embrace the chance to grow stronger with new relationships. It's about not giving the past more power than it deserves. You can be present in the lives of those you care for by acknowledging that the past has shaped you, but not allowing it to dictate your future is more important. You create a space where old pains don't hold you back; you grow and flourish from those experiences. It isn't about erasing your past but ensuring it doesn't define your relationships. You can build a new story filled with love, respect, and mutual growth. Be happy knowing that it's okay to walk away from the pain, leaving the past behind you.

Keeping Independence: The Significance of Personal Space

In relationships, having space for ourselves is essential, even when together. Spending time apart and together strengthens the relationship, giving each of us a chance to be ourselves while still being part of something special. When we're alone, we have some of our most important conversations—with ourselves. These moments help us remember what matters most and set our goals straight. Without this time alone, relationships can distract us from our true selves. So, taking time for yourself can help with focus and strengthen your bond with your partner when you come back together. This balance changes over time as our relationships grow. Spending time alone allows us to grow as individuals and brings us closer together as a couple.

In a good relationship, we have our interests and hobbies alongside what we do together. Each of us grows and learns, making us feel good about ourselves and our relationships. It's about staying true to who we are within our relationship and knowing it's okay to have our own space. Overcoming this takes some work, but keeping our connection strong is worth it. Love and the desire to be with someone is a great feeling, but having the balance of having our own space is important. Have you ever had a friend who was all about self-love, hanging out with friends, and just doing fun stuff with others? Then, they got into a relationship, and you slowly saw them change in routine and personality, which gave you less time to spend with them. We've all had that friend. Sometimes, getting so caught up in a relationship causes people to lose their sense of who they are and who they were before they went into that relationship. Yes, being in love is beautiful, but balance is the most precious thing a human being can cherish while maintaining their identity. It's about finding a balance between being together and being independent. Keeping communication open and respecting each other's individuality is vital to building a solid relationship.

Continuous Growth: The Journey Never Ends

In relationships, growth is more than just sharing experiences; it's about growing together as individuals and together. It's a promise for the future, a commitment to becoming the best versions of ourselves, both on our own and as a team. Love isn't stagnant; it's a journey filled with new ideas, challenges, and growth opportunities. It's about embracing change and evolving together, creating a life full of exciting transformations. Staying the same goes against our nature. Holding onto the past only leads to misunderstandings. Those who embrace change on this journey aren't the same people they were when they started. This reality requires flexibility and a bond to withstand life's surprises. Growth means letting go of old habits and learning new ones.

As you learn from this book, know that relationships will always be complicated, but what matters the most is the support we give one another as we embrace the journey. Whether it is with family, coworkers, partners, or friends, understanding the dreams of others and helping each other reach them is extremely important. Celebrating milestones together, recognizing their journey, and eagerly looking forward to the road ahead is vital as we grow into denying toxicity in our environment. In a relationship's story, commitment to growth is the thread that holds it together. It's what keeps the relationship alive and ready to face any challenges. As we turn the page to a new chapter, we commit to walking this journey hand in hand, prepared for whatever comes our way.

Chapter Eight
CONCLUSION

A s we've approached the end of this book, let's take a moment to celebrate the journey we've shared. We've delved into the depths of toxic relationships, explored their complexities, and uncovered ways to heal and prevent them. Throughout our discussions, we've focused on empowering you with tools and insights to embrace your past and pave the way for a brighter future. A recurring theme in our dialogue has been the idea of recovery. It's not just about escaping toxicity; it's about thriving and nurturing meaningful connections. And you have made significant strides on this path of recovery. Your progress is an example of hope for others.

This journey of empowerment relies on your autonomy, self-belief, and the courage to create positive change, surrounding yourself only with those who truly value and support you. I want to extend an invitation for you to share your own story and feedback. Doing so makes you part of a community of brave souls navigating their paths from darkness to light, from toxicity to health. Your experiences, no matter how small, serve as an example of hope and strength for others on similar journeys.

Lastly, I express my deepest gratitude for entrusting me with your journey. Facing and overcoming toxic relationships demands immense courage, and by opening this book and your heart to the possibility of change and growth, you've taken a monumental step forward. Remember, you're never alone on this path. We can build a future filled with healthier relationships, deeper connections, and boundless joy. Thank you for allowing me to walk alongside you. Here's to your continued growth, healing, and happiness.

REFERENCES

Flintoff, S. (2023, October 3). *You Should Update Privacy Settings on All of Your Apps. Here's Why*. Retrieved June 2024.

Gallo, A. (2023). *What Is Active Listening?* Retrieved June 3, 2024, from What Is Active Listening? Retrieved June 2024.

Lovelace, R. 2001. Dynamics of spiritual development . Ransom House, p. 277.

Pluut, H., & Wonders, J. (2020). Not Able to Lead a Healthy Life When You Need It the Most: Dual Role of Lifestyle Behaviors in the Association of Blurred Work-Life Boundaries With Well-Being. *Frontiers in psychology*, *11*, 607294.

Robinson, S. (2023). 5 Easy Steps to Start a Conversation (Engage Like a Pro!) - Relationships - eNotAlone. Retrieved June 2024.

RESOURCES

- *Gaslighting: What it is, long-term effects, and what to do* https://www.medicalnewstoday.com/articles/long-term-effects-of-gaslighting

- *15 Signs of Love Bombing - And What to Do About It* https://www.choosingtherapy.com/love-bombing/

- *Covert Narcissism: Recognizing Subtle Signs in ...* https://www.centerforsharedinsight.com/blog/covert-narcissism-recognizing-subtle-signs-relationships/46143

- *The Cycle Ends Here - A Domestic Abuse Survivor's Story* https://hernexxchapter.org/blog/2019/10/22/the-cycle-ends-here-a-domestic-abuse-survivors-story/

- *How To Heal From Emotional Abuse: The Ultimate Guide To ...* https://eddinscounseling.com/how-to-heal-from-emotional-abuse/

- *What Is The Best Therapy for Narcissistic Abuse?* https://www.charliehealth.com/post/what-is-the-best-therapy-for-narcissistic-abuse

- *Setting Healthy Boundaries in Relationships - HelpGuide.or g* https://www.helpguide.org/articles/relationships-communic ation/setting-healthy-boundaries-in-relationships.htm

- *How to Use Mindfulness to Ease and Heal Trauma* https://www.healthline.com/health/how-trauma-informed-min dfulness-helps-me-heal-from-the-past-and-cope-with-the-presen t

- *Relationships and communication - Better Health Channel* https://www.betterhealth.vic.gov.au/health/healthyliving/relati onships-and-communication#:~:text=be%20clear%20about%20 what%20you,want'%20and%20'I%20feel'

- *18 Best Self-Esteem Worksheets and Activities (Incl. PDF)* https://positivepsychology.com/self-esteem-worksheets/

- *9 tips for setting healthy boundaries — Calm Blog* https://www.calm.com/blog/9-tips-for-set-ting-healthy-boundaries

Printed in Great Britain
by Amazon

58061955R00088